WILD DEMOCRACY

Degrowth, Permaculture, and the Simpler Way

WILD DEMOCRACY

Degrowth, Permaculture, and the Simpler Way

Samuel Alexander
Collected Essays Volume III

WILD DEMOCRACY: DEGROWTH, PERMACULTURE, AND THE SIMPLER WAY

Published by the Simplicity Institute, Melbourne, 2017
www.simplicityinstitute.org

Cover image by Maria Pena © 2017
Cover design by Guillem Mari © 2017

ISBN 978-0-9941606-6-9 (paperback ISBN)

Advance praise for *Wild Democracy*

'*Wild Democracy* is a daring and compelling collection of essays that explores the theory and practice of moving towards an equitable, post-growth society, and defends an alternative, post-consumerist account of human flourishing. Thoreau believed that 'in wildness lies the preservation of the world' and Samuel Alexander has shown us how we do this in our back-yards, our local communities and our everyday practices. He has done Thoreau proud.'

– Robyn Eckersley, author of
The Green State: Rethinking Democracy and Sovereignty

'Building bridges between different schools of thought, Samuel Alexander outlines an alternative view to the nightmare of a growth society racing towards collapse, articulating various post-capitalist approaches, between anarcho-marxism, wild democracy and spirituality. In doing so this book attempts to overcome the old divide between reformism and revolution.'

– Serge Latouche, author of *Farewell to Growth*

CONTENTS

ACKNOWLEDGEMENTS

The chapters of this book have been published elsewhere in slightly revised versions. Details of publication and co-authorship are noted below.

Chapter One was first published as 'Policies for a Post-Growth Economy' (MSSI Issues Paper, April 2016).

Chapter Two, co-authored with Jacob Garrett, was first published as 'The Moral and Ethical Weight of Voluntary Simplicity' (Simplicity Institute Report, 17a, 2017).

Chapter Three, co-authored with Jonathan Rutherford, is to be published as 'The Transitions Towns Movement as Model for Urban Transformation' in Moore, T., de Haan, F., Home, R., and Gleeson, B (eds). *Urban sustainability transitions: Australian cases – international perspectives.* Japan: Springer (forthcoming 2017).

Chapter Four, co-authored with John Wiseman, was first published as 'The degrowth imperative: Reducing energy and resource consumption as an essential component in achieving carbon budget targets' in Garcia, E., Mertinez-Iglesias, M, and Kirby, P (eds). *Transitioning to a Post-Carbon Society: Degrowth, Austerity, and Wellbeing.* Palgrave Macmillan, London. Chapter 4, pp. 87–108.

Chapter Five, co-authored with Mark A. Burch, is to be published as 'Voluntary simplicity and the steady state economy' in Washington, H. *Positive Steps to a Steady State Economy* (2017, forthcoming).

Chapter Six was first published as 'Frugal abundance in an age of limits: Envisioning a degrowth society' in Garcia, E., Mertinez-Iglesias, M., and Kirby, P. (eds) *Transitioning to a*

Post-Carbon Society: Degrowth, Austerity, and Wellbeing. Palgrave Macmillan, London. Chapter 7, pp 159–179.

Chapter Seven was first published as 'Wild democracy: A bio-diversity of resistance and renewal' (Simplicity Institute Report, 16a, 2016). An excerpt was also published in *Adbusters* (Nov/Dec, 2016, #128). A revised version, co-authored with Peter Burdon, will appear in *The Ecological Citizen* in 2017.

Chapter Eight was first published as 'A prosperous descent: Telling new stories as the old book closes' in Alexander, S. and Adcock, B. *Imagining the Future: Notes from the Frontier* (*Griffith Review*, 52, pp 4–24).

I am grateful for the opportunity to reprint.

I would also like to acknowledge the work and encouragement of my editor, Antoinette Wilson, and cover designer, Guillem Mari. Thank you both again for your generous efforts. The beautiful cover image was created by Maria Pena, who generously gave me permission to use it. I'd like to thank Esther Alloun and Guillaume Dutilleux for assistance translating the review from Serge Latouche. Finally, I would like to express deepest thanks to the Melbourne Sustainable Society Institute for supporting my work for a number of years, including in the preparation of this manuscript.

INTRODUCTION

*The future is dark, with a darkness as much
of the womb as of the grave.*
– Rebecca Solnit

We are living through a moment in history when democracy is being threatened in alarming ways on various fronts. For decades the political sovereignty of nation-states has been undermined by a globalising market economy and corporate influence, whereby politicians have dared not interfere with the logic of deregulated 'free trade' and profit-maximisation for fear of capital flight. The rule of law has thus become subservient in many ways to the rule of corporations, when democracy requires the reverse. Recent digital innovations have also ushered in an age of surveillance capitalism on an unprecedented scale, such that Orwellian dystopias no longer lie in the realm of fiction. With access to 'big data' – that is, vast stores of information about our individual activity on the Internet – politicians (or politically ambitious oligarchs) are now able to hire IT firms to manipulate public consciousness with terrifying sophistication and power. The so-called 'post-truth' era has emerged at the same time, in which scientific evidence, logic, and accountability are being dangerously undermined by the likes of Donald Trump, striking another blow to the traditions of scientific and democratic discourse. To make matters worse, consumerist cultures in the West have given rise to citizenries that are broadly apolitical, seemingly happy to leave the job of governance to the economic elites and their political representatives in exchange for the promise of rising incomes. Democracy is not dead but evidently it is dying, and it is not clear where, when, or even if, social movements of resistance and renewal will emerge that are able to reverse these worrying trends. The hour is dark and a bright new dawn is not guaranteed.

All this is taking place in an age increasingly signified as 'the Anthropocene' – the first geological era caused by human impacts on the biosphere. The single-minded pursuit of economic growth has led to the flagrant disregard of environmental concerns, with planetary impacts continuing to intensify as a growing global population seeks to emulate the high-consumption lifestyles celebrated in the most developed regions of the world. Nevertheless, billions around the world remain impoverished while a privileged minority of elites have accumulated levels of wealth utterly beyond any sense of justice or decency. The richest eight men now own more than the poorest half of humanity. Pause for a moment, if you have the courage, and let that statistic sink in. Shouldn't this make us furious to the point of revolution? Or must we accept this as 'just the way the world is'? The great multitudes that are marginalised by global capitalism are a dynamite class that must be carefully managed by those in power in order to maintain the established order.

Well-worn appeals to technological solutions, 'green growth', and the efficiency of free markets seem coherent in theory – logically consistent within the flawed paradigm of neoclassical economics – yet despite decades of promises about 'sustainable development' the biosphere continues to be degraded violently, with dire implications that are in the process of unfolding across the globe. It seems a rising tide is destined to sink all boats. The climate continues to destabilise as fossil fuel consumption, industrial agriculture, and deforestation remain accepted practices; non-renewable resources continue to deplete; peak oil looms; biodiversity is in terminal decline, and the march of Empire continues to reach into the furthest corners of Earth in search of trees, animals, minerals, land, and labour to commodify and exploit. How humanity manages the geopolitical tensions that will inevitably arise as resource scarcity bites harder in coming years will surely define what shape the 21st century ultimately takes.

Despite the fact that the global economy is in the process of committing ecocide, capitalism has a structural imperative to pursue growth without limit. It must grow or the system begins to fray. Moreover, this structural growth imperative is reflected socially in the fetishistic attitudes that have developed in consumer cultures toward money, affluence, fame, and status, as if Kim Kardashian epitomised a life well lived. No matter how rich a society or individual becomes, the dominant strains of political and economic discourse hold out more economic growth and rising levels of affluence as the only conceivable solutions to the problems that persist. Apparently only more growth can solve the problems that growth has caused – a claim made with straight faces by mainstream economists who seem genuinely oblivious to the contradiction at the heart of their worldview. They are like the snakes that are seen eating their own tails, embodying the ideology of the cancer cell.

Nevertheless, the fact that the growth economy has begun to fail on its own terms, every day threatening the onset of GFC 2.0, has still not provoked any broad criticism of the basic goal of globalising debt-ridden consumerism – the only conception of 'utopia' permitted within the ideological confines of global capitalism. And it is now trite to repeat the dictum that it is easier to imagine the end of the world than the end of capitalism. Certainly, one is tempted to despair.

One might insist that this lack of imagination is astounding and unforgivable, but as the Parisian graffiti of May '68 stated: 'Those who lack imagination cannot imagine what is lacking.' This may ultimately prove to be the most suitable epitaph to place on the gravestone of industrial civilisation as it continues its inevitable descent in coming years and decades. The challenge for humanity is now the challenge of managing this descent as wisely, compassionately, and creatively as possible, knowing that the transition 'beyond' will likely be punctuated with a series of crises as the new world takes form – in one way or another. We should aim for sustainability, of course, but may have to settle for resilience.

As the poet-farmer Wendell Berry notes with characteristic wisdom: 'We don't have a right to ask whether we are going to succeed or not; the only question we have a right to ask is: "What's the right thing to do?"'

◆ ◆ ◆

In this third volume of my collected essays I continue developing the lines of argument presented in the earlier volumes, *Prosperous Descent: Crisis as Opportunity in an Age of Limits* (2015) and *Sufficiency Economy: Enough, for Everyone, Forever* (2015). I situate my work in that small space in which the systemic critique of capitalism overlaps with a deep green environmentalism. This space is small because most in the environmental movement do not seem to appreciate the systemic need to transcend capitalism, and most Leftist critics of capitalism do not seem to appreciate that 'growth socialism' (with a broader distribution of wealth) is no more sustainable than 'growth capitalism' (with its highly concentrated distribution of wealth). A small number of us are working on the narrow intersection of these worldviews, where it is recognised that social justice and the severe environmental limits on a full planet necessitate, in the developed world, a degrowth transition of planned economic contraction, informed by the values and visions of democratic eco-socialism, permaculture, voluntary simplicity, and an economics of sufficiency. At the same time, I am often struck by the realisation that the vision of material sufficiency that informs all my work would remain even in the absence of current environmental and humanitarian crises. The good life does not consist in the consumption and accumulation of ever more 'nice things'. In the end, I believe human beings seek a deeper connection to each other and to nature than what is provided in consumer cultures, and the good news is that this post-materialist form of flourishing does not have to cost the Earth. This realisation is the source of grounded hope that keeps despair at the door.

While I have structured the following chapters deliberately

and feel they are best read in order, each chapter stands on its own well enough, so readers should feel free to jump around depending on interest. Below I provide an overview of the book, through which the key themes and perspectives are introduced.

The opening chapter provides an overview of the 'limits to growth' debate and presents a summary case for why, despite the ongoing controversy, there are in fact limits to growth – ecological, energy, financial, and even social limits that are in the process of tightening their grip on the global economy. In making this case I respond to the techno-optimists and free marketeers who continue to assume blindly that technological advancement and pricing mechanisms can save the growth paradigm from itself. Some simple arithmetic demonstrates that ongoing compound growth of the global economy cannot be made sustainable: the degree of decoupling required soon becomes implausible. Accordingly, this chapter proceeds to outline a range of bold policy proposals that would be necessary (though not sufficient) to produce a stable, flourishing, post-growth economy. The chapter concludes by asking some hard questions about the transition to a post-growth economy in an attempt to deepen the understanding of the cultural and political obstacles that lie in the way.

One of the deepest cultural implications of moving toward a post-growth or degrowth economy is the fact that high-consumption, affluent lifestyles must be transcended. There is absolutely no way that our finite planet could withstand all seven-and-a-half billion people living Western-style lifestyles (to say nothing of the nine billion people expected by mid-century), nor are such lifestyles consistent with a transition beyond growth. A consumerist culture both demands and is driven by the economics of growth. Conversely, the only culture of consumption consistent with a degrowth economy is a culture of voluntary simplicity – a culture committed to living better on less. Therein lies the political significance of the voluntary simplicity movement: it must expand, radicalise, and organise in order to provide the cultural conditions necessary for a politics and macroeconomics of degrowth to emerge 'from below'.

Exploring these issues from a different angle, Chapter Two provides a philosophical rather than political examination of voluntary simplicity from a range of moral and ethical perspectives, including Peter Singer's moral theory, utilitarianism, Kantianism, virtue ethics, Christianity, and Michel Foucault's notion of an 'aesthetics of existence'. Despite the deep differences between these schools of thought, it is shown that there is a remarkable consensus on a key point: in an age of ecological overshoot, global poverty, and consumer malaise, affluent lifestyles are highly dubious from a moral and ethical perspective. Put otherwise, there are compelling reasons to be exploring post-consumerist lifestyles of reduced and restrained consumption, not only for environmental and social justice reasons, but also for the sake of advancing our own happiness and wellbeing, in both the long and short term. The central conclusions are that the ethos of voluntary simplicity should be informing and shaping our social education far more than it does, and that the casual acceptance of consumer cultures should be more explicitly and regularly challenged.

Chapter Three moves beyond the personal perspective of voluntary simplicity to explore the social significance of the permaculture and transition town movements, with a specific focus on urban transformation via grassroots activism. It is now widely accepted that recent decades of urban development, especially in the developed regions of the world, have created various deep problems from environmental and social perspectives. These include poorly designed transport and energy systems, as well as urban sprawl, inefficient building design, and a lack of public, green spaces. These design and development inadequacies are recognised as creating structural constraints that in many ways lock individuals and communities into high-impact, carbon-intensive ways of living. This poses a critically important and increasingly urgent question of how to 'transition' to alternative urban landscapes that facilitate the emergence of less impactful, low-carbon ways of living. Do we wait for governments to solve these problems? Or might we have to get active at the grassroots level and drive the change ourselves? This chapter provides a critical analysis of the emerging transition towns movement, which provides one of the more promising social movements to emerge during the last decade in response to overlapping energy, environmental, and economic crises. In doing so the analysis acknowledges its debts to the holistic design philosophy of permaculture.

In particular, permaculture theorist and educator David Holmgren – whose work has significantly shaped the transition movement – has been calling for grassroots movements to 'retrofit the suburbs'. Such a process would involve individuals and communities acting locally – with or without government support – to try to radically transform their urban landscapes by thinking creatively about how to make the best of an infrastructure that is often poorly designed from social and environmental perspectives. Defining activities include attempts to localise food production and connect with local farmers; increase home-based economies; relearn the skills of self-sufficiency; practise frugality and voluntary simplicity to reduce consumption; organise sharing and barter schemes beyond the formal economy; take the energy efficiency of their homes and lifestyles into their own hands; as well as attempt to decarbonise energy use not only through household and community-based renewable energy systems but also by minimising energy consumption through behaviour change (e.g., cycling more and driving less). Drawing on Holmgren's work, this chapter includes a visioning exercise that describes a transformed urban context looking back from the year 2030. Once more the chapter concludes by considering the obstacles that lie in the way of such a transition.

Chapter Four examines the case for degrowth through the specific lens of climate change, focusing on the most developed regions of the world. Every few months we read about high-profile studies that triumphantly declare that responding to climate change does not have to impact on economic growth (in terms of GDP) and that decarbonising the economy can even be good for GDP. While almost everyone accepts that business-as-usual cannot persist, very few people seem prepared to entertain the idea that an adequate response to climate change may actually necessitate moving beyond the growth paradigm.

The basic argument in this chapter is that the depth and speed of decarbonisation required for a safe climate is inconsistent with continuous growth in production and consumption. If the wealthy nations are to leave a fair share of the global carbon budget to the poorest nations, then planned economic contraction – or degrowth – is the most coherent economic paradigm for facilitating that climate response within those wealthy nations. Regrettably, this approach does not get a hearing in national or international political discourse – so every year the carbon budget for a safe climate continues to disappear as the world continues to pursue growth without limit. It may be that the time has passed in which we can avoid dangerous climate change, however that is not a call for inaction or despair but a call for bolder and more imaginative responses to this defining challenge of our era. As the narrator implores in the 2009 film *Home*: 'it's too late to be a pessimist'.

Chapter Five explores the political and macroeconomic significance of voluntary simplicity (noted in passing above). While voluntary simplicity is generally conceived of as a personal or household living strategy, my position has always been that lifestyle change – necessary though this is – will never be enough to produce a just and sustainable world. Our problems are systemic and thus will need a systemic response. But how is that systemic change supposed to come about? Many are quick to dismiss voluntary simplicity as politically naïve – and there are certainly elements of the movement that are – but this dismissal fails to recognise that a broad societal embrace of voluntary simplicity will be required to provide the cultural conditions needed to drive the transition to a post-growth economy and make it functional and prosperous.

This issue deserves emphasis because it barely gets a mention in the post-growth literature. It is all very well for post-growth and steady-state economists to develop sophisticated macro-economic models that seek to understand how such an economy might function. This is important and necessary work.

But in this literature there has been a failure to adequately draw out the cultural implications of their models, especially in terms of radically reduced and changed consumption practices, and a related failure to recognise that there is unlikely to be a political or macroeconomic transition to a post-growth or steady-state economy until there is a culture of voluntary simplicity that demands it.

Although this chapter is relatively short, leaving many issues in need of further development, its message is important, and serves as a partial response to those who dismiss the practice of voluntary simplicity as politically ineffective. Voluntary simplicity can be defended on various personal, social, and environmental grounds, but it also has a critical political dimension: minimising consumption can liberate people (to some extent) from the 'work-to-spend' cycle, thereby carving out more time and energy to get active in our local communities, raising awareness and building a new world from the grassroots up. For this reason I would argue that the most promising revolutionary class today is no longer the Proletariat – the working class that has nothing to lose but its chains – but instead the Voluntariat – the class of people choosing to abandon the pursuit of affluence in order to explore post-consumerist forms of flourishing and non-materialistic sources of meaning and satisfaction, including the hidden joys of grassroots activism.

One of the key barriers to the cultural embrace of voluntary simplicity is the materialistic conceptions of the good life that are so dominant within growth-orientated consumerist cultures. People find it hard to imagine how a 'simpler life' of reduced or restrained consumption can be a good life, especially when constantly bombarded with cultural and institutional messages reinforcing the view that 'more is always better' and that 'growth is always good'. Chapter Six seeks to unpack the real-world implications of an alternative, post-consumerist conception of flourishing. The chapter explores how our relationships to food, housing, energy, clothing, technology, money, etc. may need to change on the path to a degrowth society. In doing so, I attempt to describe a radical alternative economic vision based on notions of simplicity, frugality, moderation, sufficiency, resilience, relocalisation, and mindfulness. This form of economy would be one that has low energy and resource requirements relative to developed economies, but which sufficiently provides for local material needs using mostly local resources, without being relentlessly driven to expand by the growth-focused logic of profit-maximisation. The ultimate goal of the analysis is to provide a deeper insight into how degrowth might be experienced in everyday life. This is important because if people cannot envision the degrowth alternative with sufficient clarity, and see it as desirable, it is unlikely that a large social movement will arise to bring a degrowth economy into existence.

Having presented a critique of consumerism and the growth economy, and spent time defending and envisioning an alternative society informed by notions of degrowth, permaculture, and voluntary simplicity, in Chapter Seven I turn my attention to the question of political strategy. What is to be done to realise the transition needed? In answering this question there are three broad schools of political thought which I consider: first, there is the strategy of bold parliamentary reform within the existing system; second, there is the eco-socialist strategy which seeks to replace the existing system (global capitalism) with varieties of environmentally-aware socialism; and third, there is the eco-anarchist strategy which rejects the tool of the state and seeks to bring about the new society through direct, participatory grassroots activity.

Each of these strategies has strengths and weaknesses and in this penultimate chapter I attempt to negotiate this thorny theoretical space by outlining a new political orientation, sensibility, and practice – a position I call 'wild democracy'. In a global tide that seems to be drifting enthusiastically toward ecocide and fascism, wild democracy signifies a radical and participatory eco-egalitarian politics that seeks to take root beyond the tired parliamentary distinctions of Left and Right, but also beyond (and yet between) the antagonistic but enriching poles of anarchism and Marxism. As I explain, wild democracy is a localised politics with a global perspective, positioning itself 'in the wild' beyond the state and yet, at times, pragmatically engaged with the state. In short, wild democracy is a revolutionary politics without a Revolution, as such – a paradox I will unpack and defend as the analysis proceeds.

This book of collected essays concludes on a rather different note, with a reflective analysis of a real-world experiment in new ways of living and being. The project that is reviewed laid down its roots after an owner of some land in Gippsland, Australia, read my book *Entropia: Life Beyond Industrial Civilisation* (2013), which is a work of utopian fiction set after the demise of industrial civilisation on an isolated island in the South Pacific. *Entropia* envisions a radically 'simple living' culture and a post-growth economy that emerged after the 'Great Disruption', describing a way of life based on material sufficiency, frugality, renewable energy, local economy, appropriate technology, and self-governance. On the final page of *Entropia* I invited any interested readers to be in touch if they wanted to try to establish a real-world demonstration project that somehow embodied the ideas, vision, and utopian ambitions of the book.

Shortly after publication I received an email from an interested landowner wanting to take up the challenge. There were also some limited funds available to get things started. In recent years we've been developing the property in collaboration with a broad and evolving community of others, and in June 2016 released a documentary about the project called *A Simpler Way: Crisis as Opportunity*, which I co-produced with Jordan Osmond of Happen Films. Within a few months the film had been viewed half a million times on YouTube (and counting), which suggests that the film is touching on issues that contemporary culture finds worthy of consideration, reaching an audience far beyond what most academics could possibly dream of. In that sense, at least, the film can be deemed a success.

While the film certainly does not provide a blueprint or template for sustainable living that could be applied independent of context (that was never our intention), it does invite people to ask challenging questions about what sustainable consumption really means in an age of severe environmental limits and still-expanding human population. The concluding essay of this book provides some theoretical context to the demonstration project and the film, and summarises the evolution of this practical, real-world exploration of radically 'simpler ways' of living.

1

POLICIES FOR A
POST-GROWTH ECONOMY

1. Introduction

The 1972 publication of *Limits to Growth* sparked a controversy that has yet to subside. This book argued that if population, resource use, and pollution kept increasing on our finite planet, eventually economies would face environmental 'limits to growth' – with potentially dire consequences. Although evidence is mounting in support of this position (Turner, 2014; Steffan *et al.*, 2015), any suggestion that nations might have to give up economic growth, or even embrace a 'degrowth' process of planned economic contraction, is typically met with fierce resistance, especially by mainstream economists. In response to such arguments, most economists tend to insist that technological innovation, better design, and market mechanisms will mean that economies can and should continue growing indefinitely.

Those counter-arguments have shaped the cultural understanding of this debate, meaning that the 'limits to growth' perspective is widely and casually dismissed as flawed. Most people, including most politicians, still believe that sustained economic growth, in terms of GDP, is necessary for societal progress, and that such growth is consistent with environmental sustainability. For example, questioning economic growth never entered the key discussions at the Paris Climate Summit in December 2015, which implies that mainstream political and economic discourse still deems continuous GDP growth not just consistent with a safe climate, but a precondition for it.

The main political implication of the growth paradigm is that governments shape policies and institutions with the aim of promoting economic growth, giving society a pro-growth structure. This is supported by consumerist cultures that seek and indeed expect ever-rising material living standards. On the flip side, any policies and institutions that would inhibit economic growth are presumptively rejected or not even given a serious hearing.

This chapter provides a summary case for why there are, in fact, limits to growth, and outlines a range of bold policy interventions that would be required to produce a stable and flourishing post-growth economy. The analysis draws on and attempts to develop a rich array of thinking from literatures including ecological economics, eco-socialism, degrowth, and sustainable consumption. For decades a huge amount has been written in critique of growth economics, but the literature on what a post-growth economy would look like, or how to get there, is far less developed. This is inhibiting the movement for change. I acknowledge that most people do not recognise the need for a post-growth economy and therefore would reject my policy proposals as unacceptable. But as the limits to growth tighten their grip on economies in coming years and decades, I believe the debate will inevitably evolve, and the question will not be *whether* a post-growth economy is required, but rather *how* to create one – by design rather than disaster.

2. Definitions

In order to be for or against 'growth' it is important to understand what that term means, so I will begin with some definitions. Growth can be understood in various ways, including:

1. An increase in the resource/energy requirements of an economy (quantitative growth);

2. An increase in the productivity per unit of resource/energy (qualitative growth);
3. An increase in Gross Domestic Product (GDP growth);
4. An increase in wellbeing or happiness (wellbeing growth).

These are all legitimate ways to understand growth but they are not synonymous. One form of growth may or may not lead to other forms of growth. Some forms of growth may have limits, others may not. Fuzzy thinking about these forms of growth has produced unnecessary confusion and disagreement.

So where does the controversy lie?

3. How the Growth Economy is Defended

Nobody is against growth in wellbeing and even economists agree that economies cannot grow quantitatively forever on a finite planet. The real 'limits to growth' controversy lies in relation to the concepts of GDP and qualitative growth.

Defenders of growth argue that there is no reason why we cannot 'decouple' GDP growth from environmental impact in such a way that avoids any perceived limits to growth. These growth advocates might acknowledge that current forms of GDP growth are not sustainable, but nevertheless argue that what we need is 'green growth'; that is, growth based in qualitative improvement not quantitative expansion.

This view is based in neoclassical economic theory. It maintains that if natural resources begin to get scarce, prices will go up, and this will set in motion two important dynamics. First of all, increased prices will dis-incentivise consumption of that resource and encourage alternatives or substitution, thus reducing demand of the scarce resource and mitigating the problem. Secondly, increased prices will incentivise the development of new technologies, new markets, or new substitutes, which will increase the production of the scarce resource, lead to its more efficient use, and provide new alternatives.

Furthermore, when markets are working properly and all the

costs of production are 'internalised', the prices that result will mean human beings will only ever consume natural resources or pollute the environment to an 'optimal' degree. From this perspective, overconsumption of resources can only result from 'market failures', so all we need to do is fix those failures and deregulate the market, and then the environment will take care of itself as the 'invisible hand' maximises overall wellbeing. For these reasons, economists tend to argue that economies will never face limits to GDP growth. Those silly limits to growth theorists just don't understand economics. Growth is good and more growth is better!

The conclusion drawn from this neoclassical code of beliefs is that all nations on the planet (including the richest) should continue pursuing growth in GDP, while aiming to decouple that growth from environmental impact by way of qualitative growth. Not only is this the dominant understanding at the national level, it shapes international discourse too, with the United Nations recently stating that 'sustained growth' is indispensable to achieving the Sustainable Development Goals. I beg to differ.

4. The Case for a Post-Growth Economy

Such arguments for why there are no limits to growth are often coherent in theory, but when applied to practice their flaws become evident. In *Prosperity without Growth*, for example, Tim Jackson (2009) showed that if developed nations were to grow GDP by 2% over coming decades and by 2050 the global population had achieved a similar standard of living, the global economy would be 15 times larger than it is today in terms of GDP. If the global economy grew at 3% from then on it would be 30 times larger than the current economy by 2073, and 60 times larger by the end of this century.

Given that the global economy is already in gross ecological overshoot, it is utterly implausible to think that planetary eco-systems could withstand the impacts of a global economy that was 15, 30, or 60 times larger, in terms of GDP, than it is today. Even a global economy twice or four times as big should be of profound ecological concern. What makes this growth trajectory all the more implausible is that if we asked politicians whether they would prefer 4% GDP growth to 3%, they would all say yes, and the exponential growth scenario just outlined would become even more absurd. Gaia forbid we get what we are aiming for!

Yes, we need to do our very best to decouple GDP from environmental impact via qualitative growth, by exploiting appropriate technology and implementing smart design. That is absolutely necessary to achieve sustainability. And there is huge potential for efficiency improvements both in terms of cleaner production, increased recycling, and less-impactful consumer choices. Nobody is denying that. But when we think through the basic arithmetic of growth it becomes perfectly clear that compound GDP growth quickly renders the growth model a recipe for ecological and thus humanitarian disaster. We need an alternative model of economic progress, as well as a culture and set of institutions that facilitate a transition 'beyond growth'.

In short, the fatal problem with the growth model is that it relies on an extent of decoupling that quickly becomes unachievable. We simply cannot make a growing supply of food, clothes, houses, cars, appliances, gadgets, etc. with 15, 30, or 60 times less energy and resources than we do today. To make matters worse for the defenders of 'green growth', research published in 2015 by the US Proceedings of the National Academy of Sciences (Wiedmann *et al.*, 2015) has debunked the widespread myth that the developed nations are already in process of significant decoupling. It turns out that what developed nations have mainly been doing is outsourcing energy- and resource-intensive manufacturing and 'recoupling' it elsewhere, especially China. The consequence is that as the world naïvely pursues green growth, the environmental crisis continues to worsen. Technology and 'free markets' are not the salvation they promised to be.

In order to move toward a just and sustainable global economy, the developed nations must reduce their resource demands to a 'fair share' ecological footprint – which might imply an 80%

reduction or more (depending on the resource and context) – if the global population is to achieve a similar material living standard. But such significant quantitative reductions cannot be achieved if we persist with the dominant economics of GDP growth. It follows that the developed nations need to initiate policies for a post-growth economy at once, and in time the developing nations will also need to transition to a post-growth economy, so that the global economy comes to operate within the sustainable carrying capacity of the planet while providing a sufficient material standing of living for all people. This is humanity's defining challenge in coming years and decades.

5. Policies for a Post-Growth Economy

As outlined below, a post-growth economy will require, among other things, developing new macroeconomic policies and institutions, confronting the population challenge, and culturally embracing post-consumerist lifestyles of material sufficiency. The following proposals are not intended to be comprehensive, and they are not presented as a blueprint that could be applied independent of context. Instead, the review simply outlines a range of key issues that would need to be addressed in any 'top down' transition to a post-growth economy. After outlining what the structures of a post-growth economy might look like, I consider the question of whether such an economy could be legislated into existence in a globalised market economy, or whether post-growth economics is inconsistent with globalisation as we know it.

5.1 Explicit adoption of post-growth measures of progress

In order to transcend the growth model, the first thing needed is to adopt better and more nuanced measures of progress than GDP (Stiglitz, Sen, and Fitoussi, 2010). What we measure, and how we measure it, matters. It is now widely recognised that GDP is a deeply flawed measure of societal progress, yet it remains the dominant way to assess politico-economic success. GDP is merely an aggregate of market transactions, making no distinction between economic activities that contribute positively to sustainable wellbeing and those that diminish it. For example, GDP can be growing while at the same time our environment is being degraded, inequality is worsening, and social wellbeing is stagnant. Accordingly, a politics and economics 'beyond growth' must begin by explicitly adopting some post-growth measure of progress, such as the Genuine Progress Indicator (GPI). Although it is not a perfect metric, the GPI takes into account a wide range of social, economic, and environmental factors that GDP ignores, thus representing a vast improvement over GDP. Public understanding of and support for such post-growth accounting systems would open up political space for political parties to defend policy and institutional changes – such as those outlined below – which would genuinely improve social wellbeing and enhance ecological conditions, even if these would not maximise growth in GDP. If we do not measure progress accurately, we cannot expect to progress.

5.2 Reduce overconsumption via diminishing 'resource caps'

One of the defining problems with the growth paradigm is that the developed nations now have resource and energy demands that could not possibly be universalised to all nations. The quantitative 'scale' of our economies is overblown. It follows that any transition to a just and sustainable world requires the developed nations to stop overconsuming the world's scarce resources and reduce resource and energy demands significantly. Although in theory efficiency gains in production provide one pathway to reduced demand, the reality is that within a growth economy, efficiency gains tend to be reinvested in more growth and consumption, rather than reducing impact. After all, efficiency gains can reduce the costs of production, making a commodity cheaper, thus incentivising increased consumption of the commodity. In order to contain this well documented phenomenon (for a review, see Alexander, 2015: Ch. 1), a post-growth economy would need to introduce diminishing resource caps – that is, well defined limits to resource consumption – to ensure that efficiency gains are directed into reducing overall resource consumption, not directed into more growth. In fact, diminishing resource caps would actually encourage and stimulate efficiency improvements, because producers would know that there would be increasing competition over key resources and so would be driven to eliminate waste and create a 'circular economy' where products at the end of their life are reused in the next phase of production. In an age of ecological over-shoot, the overconsuming developed nations need to achieve significant absolute reductions in resource demand (absolute decoupling) not just productivity gains (relative decoupling). Determining where to set the resource caps, how quickly they should be reduced (e.g., 3% per year to allow markets to adjust), and where they should be aiming to stabilise (e.g., an equal per capita share), are open questions that can be debated. Formulating a workable policy in this domain would require, among other things, a highly sophisticated and detailed scientific accounting of resource stocks and flows of the economy. But the first step is simply to recognise that, in the developed nations, diminishing resource caps are a necessary part of achieving the 'degrowth' in resource consumption that is required for justice and sustainability.

5.3 Working hour reductions

One obvious implication of diminishing resource caps is that a lot less resource-intensive producing and consuming will take place in a post-growth economy. That will almost certainly mean reduced GDP, although there is still great scope for qualitative growth (technological innovation and efficiency improvements). But what implications will a contracting economy have for employment? Growth in GDP is often defended on the grounds that it is required to keep unemployment at manageable levels. If a nation gives up the pursuit of GDP, therefore, it must maintain employment via some other means. Restructuring the labour market is essential for the stability of any post-growth economy. Today, Australians work some of the longest hours in the OECD, but it is not clear such long hours contribute positively to social wellbeing. Could we work less but live more? By reducing the average working week to, say, 28 hours, a post-growth economy would share the available work amongst the working population, thereby minimising or eliminating unemployment even in a non-growing or contracting economy, while at the same time increasing social wellbeing by reducing overwork (Coote and Franklin, 2013). The aim would be to systematically exchange superfluous consumption for increased free time, which would also bring environmental benefits. While some of the increased free time could be spent enjoying local, low-impact leisure activities, some of it would also be spent engaging in the informal economy, such as activities of self-sufficiency (e.g., various forms of household production, growing food, house maintenance, sharing, volunteering, etc.) and local barter. This increased self-sufficiency and community engagement would also mitigate the impacts of reduced income in a post-growth economy by reducing household expenditure on basic needs. In this way a post-growth economy would not induce spiralling unemployment or hardship as is often feared. A deliberately created post-growth or degrowth economy is very different to unplanned recession. Indeed, planned contraction of the formal economy has the potential to liberate people from the work-to-spend cycle and provide people with more autonomy, meaning, and variety in their working lives.

5.4 Rethink budget spending for a post-growth transition

Governments are the most significant player in any economy and have the most spending power. Accordingly, if governments decide to take the limits to growth seriously this will require a fundamental rethink of how public funds are invested and spent. Broadly speaking, within a post-growth paradigm public spending would not aim to facilitate sustained GDP growth but instead fund the projects and infrastructure needed to support a swift transition to a post-growth economy. This would include huge divestment from the fossil fuel economy and a co-relative reinvestment in renewable energy systems (see next section). But it would also require huge investment in other forms of 'green' infrastructure. The importance of creating new infrastructure highlights the fact that consumption practices in a society do not take place in a vacuum. Instead, our consumption takes place within structures of constraint, and those structures make some lifestyle options easy or necessary, and other lifestyle options difficult or impossible. Currently, many people find themselves 'locked in' to high-impact lifestyles due to the structures within which they live their lives (Sanne, 2002). To provide one example: it is very difficult to stop driving a private motor vehicle if there is poor public transport and insufficient bike lanes. Change the infrastructure, however, and new, low-impact lifestyles implied by a post-growth economy would be more easily embraced. Greening infrastructure will therefore require a significant revision of government expenditure. Recognising climate change as a national 'security threat', for example, and on that basis redirecting a significant portion of military spending toward renewable energy and efficient systems of public transport, is one path to funding the infrastructure (and other post-growth policies) needed for a stable and flourishing post-growth economy. In short, how a government spends its money is how it votes on what kind of world it desires.

5.5 Renewable energy

In anticipation of the foreseeable stagnation and eventual decline of fossil fuel supplies, and recognising the grave dangers presented by climate change, a post-growth economy would need to transition swiftly to renewable energy and more efficient energy systems and practices. This provides a hugely promising space to meaningfully employ large segments of the population as the fossil fuel economy enters terminal decline. But just as important as 'greening' the supply of energy is the challenge (too often neglected) of reducing energy demand. After all, it will be much easier to transition to 100% renewable energy if energy use is significantly reduced through behavioural changes, reduced production and consumption, and more efficient appliances. Indeed, the extremely tight and fast diminishing carbon budget for a safe climate now makes this 'demand side' response a necessity (Anderson, 2013; Anderson, 2015), yet the significantly reduced energy demand required for a safe climate is incompatible with the growth model, because energy is what drives economic growth (see Ayres and Warr, 2009). Accordingly, a post-growth politics would initiate a transition to 100% renewable energy financed in part by a strong carbon tax, and undertake a public education campaign to facilitate reduced energy demand. Given how hard it will be to fully replace the fossil fuel economy with renewable energy (especially the 94 million barrels of oil currently consumed everyday), it is also worth highlighting that a post-carbon economy will have to adapt to an energy descent context and is likely to be a far more localised economy than the globalised, fossil fuel-dependent economy we know today (Moriarty and Honnery, 2008). While there would still be some limited space for global trade in a post-growth economy, most production would seek, by default, to use local resources from the bioregion to meet mostly local needs, thereby shortening the links between production and consumption. As well as running the economy on renewables, a post-growth strategy could also involve placing a moratorium on the cutting down of old growth forests and planting up huge tracts of land with trees to sequester carbon. Any coherent climate strategy must also address the huge carbon footprint of meat (especially red meat) and accordingly promote significantly reduced meat consumption (see Harvey, 2016).

5.6 Banking and finance reform

Currently, our systems of banking and finance essentially have a 'growth imperative' built into their structures. Money is loaned into existence by private banks as interest-bearing debt, and in order to pay back that debt plus the interest, an expansion of the money supply is required (Trainer, 2011). Furthermore, there is so much public and private debt today that the only way it could be paid back is via decades of continued GDP growth. This type of banking system requires growth for stability and yet limitless economic growth, as argued above, is the driving force behind the environmental crisis. In order to move toward a stable, post-growth economy, part of the institutional restructuring required involves deep reform of banking and finance systems. This is a complex transition that could take various forms, but at base it would require the state taking responsibility for creating banking and finance systems that do not require growth for stability, and strictly regulating these systems to ensure equity. A post-growth transition might also require 'debt jubilees' in some circumstances, especially in developing nations that are unjustly being suffocated by interest payments to creditors in the rich world. Developing nations, for example, receive about $136 billion in aid from donor countries but pay about $600 billion servicing debt (see Hickel, 2013). No fancy theorising can plausibly defend such a situation as just.

5.7 Population policies

As population grows, more resources are required to provide for the basic material needs of humanity (food, clothing, shelter, etc.), increasing our demands on an already overburdened planet. It is absolutely imperative that nations around the world unite to confront the population challenge directly, rather than just assuming that the problem will be solved when the developing world gets rich. Population policies will inevitably be controversial but the world needs bold and equitable leadership on this issue. Research suggests that the world is facing a population of around 9.5 billion by mid-century and 11 billion by the end of this century (Gerland *et al.*, 2014), which would be utterly catastrophic from both social and environmental perspectives. As Paul Ehrlich famously noted, 'whatever problem you're interested in, you're not going to solve it unless you also solve the population problem.' The first thing needed is a global fund that focuses on providing the education, empowerment, and contraception required to minimise the estimated 87 million unintended pregnancies that occur every year (WHO, 2016). If these unplanned pregnancies were avoided, a significant part of the population problem would be resolved. Furthermore, all financial incentives that encourage population growth should be abolished and the benefits of small families should be highlighted. Command-and-control policies, such as one- or two-child policies, should be a last resort, but even such controversial policies would arguably be preferable to a world of 11 billion people. I think everyone who casually dismisses the limits to growth perspective should be given a Petri dish with a swab of bacteria in it and watch as the colony grows until it consumes all the available nutrients or is poisoned by its own waste. From a distance, Earth today would look very much like that Petri dish. Bacteria mightn't show the insight to stop growing on a finite resource base – but will humanity? We are at the crossroads and are in the process of choosing our collective fate.

5.8 Reimagining the good life beyond consumer culture

Despite the environmental necessity of population stabilisation and eventual decline, the fact remains that currently there are 7.4 billion people on earth, all of whom have the right to the material conditions needed to live a full and dignified human life. Nevertheless, if the global economy is to raise the material living standards of the great multitudes currently living in destitution, this is likely to put further pressure on global ecosystems. Therefore, in order to leave some 'ecological room' for the poorest people to develop their economic capacities in some form, high-impact consumer lifestyles must be swiftly transcended and rich nations must initiate a degrowth process of planned economic contraction. There is no conceivable way that 7 billion people, let alone 11 billion, could live sustainably on Earth in material affluence. Globalising affluence, quite simply, would be ecologically catastrophic. Accordingly, members of the global consumer class need to reimagine the good life beyond consumer culture and develop new conceptions of human flourishing based on sufficiency, moderation, frugality, and non-materialistic sources of meaning and satisfaction. From a consumption perspective, this might mean driving less and cycling more; growing local organic food; putting on woollen clothing rather than always turning on the heater; taking shorter showers; flying less or not at all; eating less meat; making and mending rather than buying new; sharing more; and in countless other ways rethinking lifestyles in ways that radically reduce energy and resource burdens. In sum, a post-growth economy would not aim to provide affluence for all but modest sufficiency for all – which is what justice and sustainability requires. A necessary part of any post-growth politics would therefore require a public relations campaign that openly challenged consumerist lifestyles and highlighted the social and environmental benefits of a 'simpler life' with less stuff but more free time. Linked to such an education campaign would be a strategy to minimise exposure to advertising that currently glorifies and encourages consumerism. For example, a post-growth economy might follow the city of Sao Paulo by banning all outdoor advertising on billboards, shop fronts, vehicles, etc. What we are exposed to shapes who we are.

5.9 Distributive justice

Last but not least, environmental concerns cannot be isolated from social justice concerns. The conventional path to poverty alleviation is via the strategy of GDP growth, on the assumption that 'a rising tide will lift all boats'. Given that a post-growth economy deliberately seeks a non-growing economy – on the assumption that a rising tide will *sink* all boats – poverty alleviation must be achieved more directly, via redistribution, both nationally and internationally. In other words (and to change the metaphor), a post-growth economy would eliminate poverty and achieve distributive equity not by baking an ever-larger economic pie but by slicing it differently. Any attempt to systemically redistribute wealth via taxation or property reform will be highly controversial, especially in our neoliberal age, but present concentrations of wealth demand a political response. Research published in 2017 shows that the richest eight men on the planet now own more than the poorest half of humanity (Hardoon, 2017). Dwell on that for a moment. Furthermore, it has been shown that, as the US seeks to recover from the Global Financial Crisis, 95% of GDP growth has gone to the top 1% of the population (Saez, 2012). This highlights the point that growth itself will not resolve poverty; we need policies that directly redistribute wealth and ensure a dignified material baseline. There is no single best policy for eliminating poverty or achieving a just distribution of wealth, but key policy options include (i) a basic income for all, which guarantees every permanent resident with a minimal, living wage; (ii) an alternative is the 'negative income tax', which guarantees a minimum income for those who earn below a certain threshold; (iii) progressive tax policies (i.e., the more you earn, the higher the tax rate), which could culminate in a top tax rate of 90% or more; (iv) wealth taxes, that systematically transfer 3% of private wealth from the richest to the poorest, recognising the large social component in wealth production; and (v) estate taxes of 90% or more to ensure the laws of inheritance and bequest do not create a class system of entrenched wealth and entrenched poverty. These and other tax-and-transfer policies should be explored to eliminate poverty and ensure distributive equity. Obviously, arguments that such policies would inhibit growth do not hold water within a post-growth framework.

I contend that these policy platforms – all in need of detailed elaboration and discussion – should be the opening moves in a 'top down' transition to a post-growth economy. To be employed in concert, they clearly challenge the dominant macroeconomics of growth and would require far more social control over the economy than neoliberal capitalism permits today. Markets work well in some circumstances, no doubt, but leaving everything to the market and thinking this will magically advance the common good has been proven dangerously false. It follows that a post-growth economy must be a post-capitalist or eco-socialist economy, with increased democratic planning and perhaps even some rationing of key resources to ensure distributive equity. The policies above also depend upon a society that sees the necessity and desirability of a post-growth economy, hence the special importance of public education campaigns and the emergence of a new, post-consumerist culture of consumption.

Beyond these policy platforms, it should go without saying that any post-growth transition would require an array of other revolutionary reforms, including policies to create (or recreate) a 'free press'; policies to ensure that campaign financing rules do not permit undue economic influence on the democratic process; policies that ensure affordable housing and access to land; policies to promote alternative corporate forms, such as worker cooperatives; and so forth. I do not pretend to have provided a complete political agenda for a post-growth economy. The proposals above are merely key aspects of such a transition and a good place to begin thinking about how to structure a just and sustainable, post-growth economy.

As well as maintaining and updating the critique of growth and detailing coherent policies for a post-growth economy, it is also important to develop sophisticated transition strategies that would maximise the chances of a post-growth political campaign succeeding. Among other things, this would involve exploring the role grassroots social movements might have to play creating the cultural foundations for a post-growth economy. As suggested above, a clever and sustained 'social marketing' campaign promoting a post-growth economy is critical here, in order to weaken the hold the ideology of growth has on society.

6. Hard Truths about a 'Top-Down' Transition

I wish to conclude by acknowledging several hard truths about the feasibility of a 'top down' transition to a post-growth economy. The first is to note that cultures around the world, especially in the developed world, are not close to being ready to take the idea of a post-growth economy seriously. In Australia, for example, our current and prospective governments are all firmly embedded in the growth paradigm and they show no signs of questioning it – none at all. At the cultural level, the expectation of ever-increasing affluence (which assumes continued growth) is as strong as ever. In this political and cultural context, the policy proposals outlined above – however necessary they might be to confronting the limits to growth predicament – will strike most people as wildly unrealistic, overly interventionist, and probably undesirable. I am not so deluded as to think otherwise.

The second point to note, subtly linked to the first, is that the powers-that-be would not tolerate these policies for a post-growth economy. To provide a case in point, when a relatively fringe Occupy Movement in 2011 began to challenge undue corporate influence on democracy and make noise about wealth inequality, soon enough the executive branches of government bore down upon the activists and stamped out the opposition. Mainstream media made little effort to understand the movement. Given that a post-growth economy would directly undermine the economic interests of the most powerful corporations and institutions in society, one should expect merciless and sustained resistance from these vested interests if a post-growth movement ever began gaining ascendency.

The third point to note – and probably the most challenging – is that, in a globalised world order, even the bold policies proposed above would be unlikely to produce a stable and flourishing post-growth economy. After all, how would the stock markets react if a government announced a policy agenda that would deliberately aim to contract the economy for environmental and social justice reasons? More specifically, how would the stock markets react if a government, in pursuit of sustainability and global equity, introduced a diminishing resource cap that sought to phase out the most damaging industries and reduce resource consumption by 80% of current Australian levels? I suspect there would be utter turmoil, ultimately leading to an economic crash far greater than the global financial crisis. My point is that it may well be impossible to implement a smooth 'top down' transition to a post-growth economy, even if a strong social movement developed that wanted this. The market economies we know today would be unlikely to be able to adjust to the types and speed of foundational changes required. A 'great disruption' of some form may be a necessary or inevitable part of the transition beyond growth.

To make matters more challenging still, in a globalised economy, it is not clear whether a single nation could adopt a post-growth economy without inducing a range of antagonistic reactions from other nations. On the one hand, there is a web of international 'free trade' agreements that make such a move highly problematic, and could even provoke sanctions from international institutions or other governments. On the other hand, in a globalised economy there is always the threat of capital flight the moment a government threatens to defy the neoliberal logic of profit-maximisation or talks of wealth redistribution. There is also the geopolitical risk of being a leader in a post-growth transition, as this may involve fewer funds available for military forces, weakening a nation's relative power globally. All of these issues radically call into question the feasibility of a 'top down' transition to a post-growth economy, and yet these challenges are rarely acknowledged in the post-growth literature.

Despite a 'top down' transition facing huge, perhaps insurmountable, obstacles, governments are going to act in one way or another, and their influence matters. It follows that we should be pressuring them to do everything they can to assist in the emergence of a post-growth economy, even if, in the end, we may need to build the post-growth economy ourselves, at the grassroots level, with or without state support.

7. Conclusion

So where does that leave us? In the paradoxical position, I would argue, of knowing that a planned transition to a post-growth economy is both necessary and seemingly impossible. If there are indeed little grounds for thinking that a 'top down' transition is likely or possible without inducing deep economic disruption and instability, one strategic deduction is that a post-growth economy, if it is to emerge, may have to be driven into existence 'from below', with local communities coming together to do it themselves. One could adopt a 'theory of change' based in anarchism or participatory democracy, in which a new, post-growth Economy B is slowly built up at the grassroots level, with active social movements more or less ignoring the state, and over time this new economy becomes dominant as the old, growth-orientated Economy A deteriorates (Trainer, 2010). Indeed, it could be argued that, at this early stage in the transition, the most important thing a concerned citizen can do is to work on changing culture at the local, community level, trusting that, over time, if a large social movement develops which demands a post-growth economy, the structures and systems necessary for such an economy will eventually filter upwards as culture radicalises and develops a more engaged political consciousness. Admittedly, these strategies are unlikely to take down Empire in the near-term, but arguably they embody a more coherent political intelligence than the conventional approach of thinking that a post-growth economy could be smoothly introduced via 'top down' parliamentary politics.

The ultimate message from this analysis, therefore, is that those concerned about limits to growth should be splitting their energies between two main activities: (1) raising awareness about the limits to growth and the inability of capitalism to resolve those limits; and (2) attempting to establish examples of the post-growth economy at the local, community level, and working on building the new systems and cultures required for such examples to proliferate and take root. Fortunately these activities are likely to help build resilience even if they fail to produce a post-growth economy. Thus, if we face a future where the growth economy grows itself to death, which seems to be the most likely scenario, then building up local resilience and self-sufficiency now will prove to be time and energy well spent. In the end, it is likely that only when a deep crisis arrives will an ethics of sufficiency come to inform our economic thinking and practice more broadly.

References

Alexander, S. 2015. *Prosperous descent: Crisis as opportunity in an age of limits*, Simplicity Institute, Melbourne.

Ayres, R. and Warr, B. 2009. *The economic growth engine: How energy and work drive material prosperity*, Edward Elgar Publishing, Cheltenham.

Anderson, K. 2013. 'Avoiding dangerous climate change demands de-growth strategies from wealthier nations', available at: http://kevinanderson.info/blog/avoiding-dangerous-climate-change-de-mands-de-growth-strategies-from-wealthier-nations/ [accessed 25 August 2015].

Anderson, K. 2015. 'Duality in climate science', *Nature Geoscience* 8, pp 898–900, DOI:10.1038/ngeo2559.

Coote, A. and Franklin, J. (eds). 2013. *Time on our side: Why we all need a shorter working week*, New Economics Foundation, London.

Elliot, L. 2016. 'Richest 62 people as wealthy as half of world's population, says Oxfam', *The Guardian* (18 January 2016), available at: http://www.theguardian.com/business/2016/jan/18/richest-62-billion-aires-wealthy-half-world-population-combined [accessed 7 March 2016].

Gerland, P. *et al.* 2014. 'World population stabilization unlikely this century', *Science* 18, September 2014, DOI: 10.1126/science.1257469.

Harvey, F. 2016. 'Eat less meat to avoid dangerous global warming, scientists say', *The Guardian* (22 March 2016), available at: http://www.theguardian.com/environment/2016/mar/21/

eat-less-meat-vegetarianism-dangerous-global-warming [accessed 22 March 2016].

Hickel, J. 2013. 'The donors' dilemma – aid in reverse: How poor countries develop rich countries', *Global Policy Journal* (12 December 2013), available at: http://www.globalpolicyjournal.com/blog/12/12/2013/donors%E2%80%99-dilemma-aid-reverse-how-poor-countries-develop-rich-countries [accessed 7 March 2016].

Jackson, T. 2009. *Prosperity without growth: Economics for a finite planet*, Earthscan, London.

Moriarty, P. and Honnery, P. 2008. 'Low-mobility: The future of transport', *Futures* 40, pp 865–872.

Saez, E. 2012. 'Striking it richer: The evolution of top incomes in the United States' (Working Paper, 3 September 2013), available at: http://eml.berkeley.edu//~saez/saez-UStopincomes-2012.pdf [accessed 7 March 2016].

Sanne, C. 2002. 'Willing consumers – or locked-in? Policies for a sustainable consumption', *Ecological Economics* 42, pp 273–287.

Steffan, W. *et al.* 2015. 'Planetary boundaries: Guiding human development on a changing planet', *Science* 347(6223), DOI: 10.1126/science.1259855.

Stiglitz, J., Sen, A., and Fitoussi, J.P. 2010. *Mis-measuring our lives: Why GDP doesn't add up*, The New Press, New York.

Trainer, T. 2010. *The transition to a sustainable and just world*, Envirobook, Sydney.

Trainer, T. 2011. 'The radical implications of a zero growth economy', *Real-World Economics Review* 57, pp 71–82.

Turner, G. 2014. 'Is collapse imminent? An updated comparison of *The Limits to Growth* with historical data', *MSSI Research Paper* No. 4, pp 1–22.

Wiedmann, T. *et al.* 2015. 'The material footprint of nations', *Proceedings of the National Academy of Sciences in the United States of America* 112(20) pp. 6271-6276, DOI: 10.1073/pnas.1220362110.

World Health Organization (WHO). 2016. 'Not every pregnancy is welcome: Planning pregnancies before they even happen', *The World Health Report*, available at: http://www.who.int/whr/2005/chapter3/en/index3.html [accessed 7 March 2016].

2

THE MORAL AND ETHICAL WEIGHT OF VOLUNTARY SIMPLICITY

1. Introduction*

A vast and growing body of scientific literature is impressing upon us that human economic activity is degrading planetary ecosystems in ways that are unsustainable. Taken as a whole, we are overconsuming Earth's resources, destabilising the climate, and decimating biodiversity (Steffan *et al.*, 2015; IPCC, 2013; WWF, 2016). At the same time, we also know that there are billions of people around the world who are, by any humane standard, under-consuming. Alleviating global poverty is likely to place even more pressure on an already over-burdened planet. To make matters worse still, the global population, currently at 7.4 billion people, is expected to rise to around 9.7 billion by mid-century and 11 billion by the end of the century (Gerland *et al.*, 2014), compounding already severe sustainability and social justice crises. Continuous economic growth seems socially necessary but ecologically disastrous (Meadows *et al.*, 2004).

What makes this entire situation more tragic still is that the high-consumption, Western-style lifestyles driving the environ-mental crisis are often failing to live up to their promise of a happy and meaningful life, leaving many people alienated from

---

* This chapter was co-authored by Samuel Alexander and Jacob Garrett.

22

their communities, disconnected from nature, unhealthy, and overworked (Hamilton and Denniss, 2005; Lane, 2000). In this context, calls by environmentalists to reject consumerist lifestyles and growth-orientated economies in favour of less impactful consumption and production practices seem powerful, even compelling, from a range of environmental, social, and even self-interested perspectives (Trainer, 2010).

Choosing to consume less while seeking a higher quality of life is a living strategy that today goes by the name 'voluntary simplicity' (Elgin, 1998; Alexander, 2009). The term was coined in 1936 by Richard Gregg (2009), a follower of Gandhi, who advocated a mindful approach to consumption which involved seeking basic material needs as directly and sustainably as possible and then directing time and energy away from limitless material pursuits in favour of exploring 'the good life' in non-materialistic sources of meaning and fulfilment. This way of life, also known as 'downshifting' or 'simple living', embraces values like moderation, sufficiency, and frugality, and eschews the materialist values of greed, acquisitiveness, luxury, and excess. By exchanging superfluous consumption for more freedom, voluntary simplicity holds out the tantalising prospect that over-consumers could live more on less (Cafaro, 2009), with positive consequences for self, others, and planet.

Despite the apparent coherency of voluntary simplicity as an appropriate response to planetary and social crises, the social movement or subculture of voluntary simplicity remains marginal. Especially in the developed regions of the world, but increasingly elsewhere, dominant consumerist cultures continue to celebrate affluence, fame, and status on the 'more is better' assumption that increased consumption is the most direct path to happiness and fulfilment (Hamilton and Denniss, 2005).

What is more, this consumerist approach to life finds a sophisticated theoretical defence in neoclassical economics, a framework which holds that pursuing self-interest in the marketplace is the best way to maximise both personal and social wellbeing. From this perspective, environmental problems only arise when prices do not accurately reflect the true costs of production (due to 'externalities'), which implies that the best way to respond to environmental problems is not to rethink consumption practices but to fix market failures from the production angle (see Princen, 2005). When prices are right, the argument goes, people will consume to an 'optimal' (utility-maximising) degree, which allegedly implies sustainability. This dominant economic perspective thus marginalises consumption as a subject of ethical concern, and based on this perspective, governments and businesses around the world argue that individuals and households should continue to consume as much as possible, because this is good for economic growth, and this paradigm assumes economic growth is the most direct path to progress (Hamilton, 2003).

Although dominant economic and cultural perspectives on consumption continue to assume that 'more is better', throughout history there have always been criticisms of materialistic values and praise given to 'simpler' ways of life (Alexander and McLeod, 2014). All the great spiritual and wisdom traditions have warned against the dangers of greed, extravagance, and acquisitiveness (see VandenBroeck, 1991), and, indeed, until quite recently, political parties across the spectrum shared a view that moderation, frugality, and humility were noble social and political values (see Shi, 2007). Nevertheless, despite this long and venerable tradition, voluntary simplicity has received surprisingly little attention from moral and ethical philosophers (see Barnett, Cafaro, and Newholm, 2005).

Accordingly, in this article, we review and examine the moral and ethical weight of voluntary simplicity from a range of philosophical perspectives, including utilitarianism, Kantianism, virtue ethics, and Christianity, in order to assess which, if any, can provide a coherent philosophical defence of voluntary simplicity. While we do not claim to present anything like an absolute philosophical foundation to voluntary simplicity, ultimately our analysis shows that voluntary simplicity can draw strong philosophical support from a surprising range of moral and ethical perspectives. Our central argument is that this overlapping support makes voluntary simplicity a robust moral and ethical position that should guide the direction of our lives and our societies much more than it does. Although we cannot detail the full complexity of the moral and ethical perspectives under consideration, and in fact we may raise as many questions as we answer, we will deem this preliminary analysis successful if it draws more attention to the crucial issues under consideration and sparks a broader discussion.

2. Affluence, Poverty, and Voluntary Simplicity

We begin our analysis with a review and application of one of the most prominent moral perspectives of recent decades: the provocative argument Peter Singer presented in his seminal paper 'Famine, Affluence, and Morality' (1972). Although Singer did not frame his argument in terms of voluntary simplicity, the weight of his reasoning provides direct moral support for this approach to life, in ways that we will explain.

The essential logic of Singer's position can be easily summarised: 1. Suffering and death from lack of food, shelter and medical care are bad from a moral perspective; 2. If it is within our power to prevent something morally bad from happening, without sacrificing anything of comparable moral importance, then morally we ought to do it. Singer argues that these principles should take no account of distance or proximity, in the sense that it should make no difference from a moral perspective whether the suffering we can prevent is near or far away.

Upon these strikingly simple and plausible premises, Singer draws very challenging conclusions. He begins illustrating the practical implications of his theory with the example of a drowning child: we can save the child, but it means getting our clothes muddy. Based on the premises stated above, morally we ought to save the child because getting our clothes muddy is morally insignificant compared to the life of the child. Who could argue with that? Surely we would all save the child out of an instinct of moral duty. The power of Singer's argument lies in how compelling this simple line of reasoning is, and yet when the implications of the theory are more broadly applied it becomes clear that many aspects of life we take for granted suddenly appear very dubious from a moral perspective. How so?

Singer's central thesis – for which he has become famous – is that people in relatively affluent societies have a moral obligation to give more of their money away to relieve the suffering of the poorest, a position that appears to follow logically if the reasoning above is accepted. Just as we should save the child because getting our clothes muddy is a relatively insignificant cost, Singer argues that many of the things we spend our money on are trivial and of limited benefit to our lives, whereas that same money could greatly reduce suffering by feeding or housing those in extreme poverty. For example, Singer argues that spending money on new clothes to look 'well dressed' does not provide for any important need: 'We would not be sacrificing anything if we were to continue to wear old clothes, and give the money to famine relief... To do so is not charitable or generous... we ought to give the money away, and it is wrong not to do so' (Singer, 1972: 699).

Suddenly many casual acts of consumption are cast in a new and questionable moral light. People might find it easy to nod their heads when Singer argues that we should save the child despite getting our clothes muddy, but the same force of logic applies to many ordinary acts of consumption whose moral legitimacy is typically unquestioned or even celebrated and admired in consumer societies. Do we really need that magazine, that new cushion, or that extra pair of shoes? Do we really need to renovate the kitchen or go on that trip to Bali? Can we justify treating ourselves to an expensive meal out or buying our children the latest plastic toy? Most people do not consider such acts immoral, but Singer's argument implies that perhaps that is moral blindness – perhaps even wilful moral blindness. Singer argues that our lives would not be significantly affected if we were to forego many such acts of consumption but we could relieve significant suffering with the money saved. Therefore, it would seem that it is our duty to forego those acts of consumption and practice voluntary simplicity in order to give more aid to the poorest around the world.

One immediate question that arises is how far to take this line of reasoning. Does the argument require us to give away everything other than what is required to meet our most basic biophysical needs? After all, if there are people who suffer greatly because they do not have those most basic needs met, perhaps all acts of consumption beyond basic needs are unjustifiable until everyone's basic needs are met. Obviously that would place a tremendously challenging moral demand on us, but that is not an argument against the validity of the demand. Indeed, it could be said that a morality that was not challenging would be no morality at all.

For present purposes, however, we feel that this boundary issue can remain unresolved without undermining our central point. While Singer's position may not be able to provide a clear-cut line between justifiable and unjustifiable consumption, his argument provides a compelling moral case that we could and should forego many acts of consumption and give the money saved to aid agencies. This could relieve great suffering without causing us any significant hardship. Indeed, according to William MacAskill (2016: 22), 'the same amount of money can do one hundred times as much benefit to the very poorest in the world as it can to benefit typical citizens of the United States [or other affluent nations].'

Perhaps part of the reason people often fail to appreciate the power of this moral position is due to the lack of proximity between acts of superfluous consumption and the individuals living in the greatest destitution. Would we be so casual in our consumption practices if we had to make our purchases before the gaze of a grossly emaciated Ethiopian child, desperate for a simple bowl of rice? Isn't that new pair of shoes morally tarnished knowing that the money spent on them could have fed that child for a month or more, perhaps saved his or her life? This is not an easy thought experiment to conduct – it can easily induce guilt, because so often we fail to live up to this standard. But by clarifying our moral obligations, we argue that this

SAMUEL ALEXANDER

line of reasoning can challenge us to rethink our consumption practices in ways that could greatly reduce human suffering. In short, Singer's argument radically calls into question the legitimacy of consumer culture and provides a robust moral case for voluntary simplicity. As the Gandhian dictum goes: 'Live simply so that others may simply live.'

3. Utilitarianism and Voluntary Simplicity

We began with Singer's argument because it is so simple, powerful, and yet challenging. The example of saving the child also makes the moral theory so tangible and practically comprehensible. We now wish to step back and consider the underlying theory of utilitarianism which subtly informs Singer's argument and which may offer further insight into possible moral foundations of voluntary simplicity.

Although the roots of utilitarianism can be found in ancient philosophers such as Epicurus, who held up happiness as the greatest good, the founding of the modern philosophic tradition of utilitarianism is typically attributed to Jeremy Bentham. The classic statement of this position was provided in Bentham's (2007 [1789]: 1) *Introduction to the Principles of Morals and Legislation*:

> Nature has placed mankind under the governance of two sovereign masters, pain and pleasure. It is for them alone to point out what we ought to do... By the principle of utility is meant that principle which approves or disapproves of every action whatsoever according to the tendency it appears to have to augment or diminish the happiness of the party whose interest is in question: or, what is the same thing in other words to promote or to oppose that happiness. I say of every action whatsoever, and therefore not only of every action of a private individual, but of every measure of government.

From this passage we can see that utilitarianism posits that the rightness or wrongness of an act is to be judged solely by its consequences, and that the only relevant factor for assessing the consequences is how much happiness or unhappiness is caused. Acting morally, therefore, implies aiming to maximise happiness and minimise unhappiness, and utilitarians tend to be egalitarian in the sense that no one's happiness counts more than anyone else's. To the objection that humans do and should value things other than the balance of happiness, utilitarians such as John Stuart Mill (2012 [1863]: 39) argue that 'happiness is desirable, and the only thing desirable, as an end; all other things being desirable as a means to that end.' We may indeed value things like health, friendship, beauty, and human rights, but classical utilitarians argue that, ultimately, we value these things because they promote happiness.

As noted in the introduction, our intention in this chapter is not to provide a comprehensive defence of utilitarianism or any of the other moral philosophies reviewed, but rather to explore what implications these theories might have on Western-style consumer practices *if* they were accepted. Accordingly, we will look no further into the various controversies still surrounding utilitarianism and instead proceed to explore whether, or to what extent, utilitarianism might provide support for voluntary simplicity.

At first instance one may have legitimate doubts about whether voluntary simplicity – choosing to live with less stuff – could maximise net happiness. After all, all Westerners and increasingly all human beings live within a globalised market society, in which individuals and governments are able to buy things that most satisfy their most pressing needs and desires – nicer clothes, a bigger house, better schools, more exotic foods, more luxurious holidays, the best healthcare, etc. More money would seem to imply more satisfaction – more happiness or 'utility' – and, indeed, the dominant economic paradigm proceeds on that assumption (Purdey, 2010).

Nevertheless, things are certainly not that simple. First of all, as noted above, throughout history there have been prophets and philosophers who have argued that true satisfaction in life does not consist in the accumulation and consumption of ever-more material things and, in fact, that materialism or consumerism implies a counter-productive approach to life that can never provide the happiness it promises. Leading examples in this tradition include figures as diverse as the Buddha, Diogenes, the Stoics, Jesus, Thoreau, and Gandhi (see Alexander and McLeod, 2014), all of whom would argue in their own way that many people could increase their happiness by giving up materialistic lifestyles and embracing lifestyles of voluntary simplicity. More recently, philosopher Kate Soper (2008) has defended voluntary simplicity as a pleasure-maximising lifestyle in terms of what she calls 'alternative hedonism'. Similarly, prominent 'degrowth' advocate, Serge Latouche (2014), defends the notion of 'frugal abundance' (see also, Trainer, 2010).

Interestingly, in recent decades a vast body of sociological and psychological literature has provided some robust empirical support for this ancient line of reasoning (e.g., Lane, 2000; Diener and Seligman, 2004; Diener, Helliwell, and Kahneman, 2010). For instance, Tim Kasser (2002) has shown that people with materialistic value-orientations (that is, people who highly value possessions and the status they bring) tend to have lower psychological wellbeing than those who are less materialistic. Richard Easterlin (1995, 2013) and others (Layard, 2005; Layard *et al.*, 2010) have provided evidence from subjective wellbeing surveys that indicate that economic growth is not increasing life satisfaction or 'evaluative happiness', particularly in the developed world. Likewise, Daniel Kahneman and Angus Deaton (2010) provide evidence that, in terms of emotional wellbeing or 'affective happiness', there seems to be a satiation point above which getting richer does not contribute to happiness. Without going into the intricacies of this diverse literature, suffice to say that there is now a compelling body of social research suggesting that many people in the most developed regions in the world are not only overconsuming from an environmental perspective but also mal-consuming from a personal wellbeing perspective.

It would seem, then, that many people living high-consumption lifestyles could actually increase their happiness – counter-intuitively perhaps – by redirecting their life energies away from materialistic pursuits and seeking the good life in non-materialistic sources of happiness. Indeed, the largest empirical survey of the voluntary simplicity movement (Alexander and Ussher, 2012) shows that 87% of people choosing to live more simply in a material sense are happier for doing so (with the other 13% being about as happy as before doing so and only a negligible amount being less happy). While most of us are exposed to advertising messages thousands of times every day imploring us to seek satisfaction through increased consumption, the modern voluntary simplicity movement, in line with ancient wisdom, is suggesting that there may be a more direct path to happiness – not by acquiring 'more' but by embracing 'enough'.

While we suggest that this 'self-interested' defence of voluntary simplicity should be taken more seriously by utilitarians, voluntary simplicity arguably has even greater moral importance to the extent it could reduce the suffering of others, both immediately and in the future. This links back to Singer's arguments. If it is the case that the pursuit of increased consumption, especially in affluent societies, is no longer increasing happiness (or at the very least no longer significantly increasing it, such that the benefit at the margin is much less than could be realised by devoting those resources to deprived persons), then the case for reducing consumption and redistributing that superfluous wealth to those in poverty becomes even stronger. Indeed, there is something morally perverse about consuming in ways that does not advance personal happiness while others suffer in material destitution.

What is more, to the extent that overconsumption of the world's resources is putting in jeopardy the viability of the planet for future generations, this also provides strong utilitarian support for voluntary simplicity. After all, if we take the happiness of future generations into account and recognise the vast suffering that would flow from ecosystemic collapse, then it would seem the moral scales fall heavily in favour of voluntary simplicity. By consuming modestly and thereby helping avoid ecosystemic collapse, we will help maintain a healthy biosphere for millions of years within which human beings can flourish; the wellbeing of millions of future generations utterly outweighs the importance (if any) of the extravagances of one present-day generation. Continuing to consume recklessly, on the other hand, is likely to lead to unfathomable suffering, with dangerous or (worse) runaway climate change being one of the greatest humanitarian threats (Gardiner, 2011).

In closing this section it is worth noting that the moral scope of utilitarianism arguably extends beyond humanity and should include, as Mill (2012 [1863] 13) argued, 'the whole of sentient creation'. That is, the entire animal kingdom, not just humans, should be included in the hedonic calculus, for as Bentham (2007 [1789] 311) asked, rhetorically: 'The question is not, Can they [animals] *reason*? nor, Can they *talk*? but Can they *suffer*?' And the answer to that final question is obviously yes – animals can suffer – and therefore morality arguably demands their consideration (Singer, 2009).

While including the concerns of non-human animals seems to rest on plausible utilitarian foundations, doing so further calls into question the legitimacy of Western-style consumption practices and the economies of growth those consumption practices both drive and depend on. A recent study (WWF, 2016) reports that over the last 40 years alone, human economic activity has reduced the populations of invertebrate species by, on average, an alarming 58%, with trends indicating that this impact will rise to 67% by 2020 if business as usual persists. Another report (Ripple *et al.*, 2016) holds that over 300 species are at grave risk of being eaten into extinction.

All this suggests that humanity, as a whole, is disregarding the moral worth of animals. Factory farming is but the most egregious example of a more general lack of moral concern. While we will not here begin to attempt to set out a complete 'solution' to this complex problem, it can be argued that a necessary *part* of any coherent and effective response will involve human beings making fewer demands on the natural habitats of Earth's declining biodiversity and taking more seriously the moral arguments for vegetarianism or veganism (Singer, 2009), or at the very least for reducing drastically our exploitation of animals, strategies which are highly consistent with a cultural embrace of voluntary simplicity.

In sum, respecting animal life provides yet further moral grounds for arguing that high-impact consumers should be embracing lifestyles of voluntary simplicity. This is part of the broader utilitarian argument contending that, if voluntary simplicity maximises happiness – human or otherwise – and minimises suffering, then living in such a way is part of what morality requires of us. From this utilitarian perspective, voluntary simplicity is morally required because it is the path to greatest net happiness for the entire community of life.

4. Kantianism and Voluntary Simplicity

It is not only in the pursuit of maximal happiness and minimal suffering that strong ethical warrant for voluntary simplicity can be found. We now begin our analysis of various non-utilitarian approaches by turning our attention to Immanuel Kant, the founder of deontological ethics. On his account, our moral duties can never be accurately derived from our fallible predictions of consequences or from how we imagine happiness might be obtained. Instead, Kant insisted that the only legitimate foundation for a system of morals is upon the universal principles of reason and their inescapable requirements of us as rational agents. Along these lines he argues that the only thing good in itself is a good will, for it alone among all other things often considered good – such as good circumstances, good temperaments, or good talents – is good apart from the ends it aims at or achieves. According to Kant, all other goods can be produced by accident without the good will of a rational agent, whereas the highest and unconditional good is sought out and produced only by good will *because it is good*, and for no other reason.

By 'good will' Kant does not mean some vague feeling of benevolence toward others, but rather that to have such a will is to have 'the ability to act according to the thought of laws' (Kant, 1785: 18), that is, the ability to act on the basis of principles and reasons. Only rational beings can do this, and so a good will is one that is motivated by the recognition of one's duty as a rational being to act according to the laws of reason. Thus if anyone fails to act in accordance with the laws of reason, he or she is not only acting irrationally, but also immorally.

In this way Kant maintains that the precepts of the rational and moral law are binding on us in ways we cannot choose to ignore: we ought to act according to the laws of reason to the extent that we are rational; to act against these laws is to shirk our inherent duty as rational beings. It is within this framework that Kant advances his famous categorical imperative, the first and most common formulation of which is, 'I ought never to act in such a way that I couldn't also will that the maxim on which I act should become a universal law' (Kant, 1785: 11). Kant takes this to be the principle of action to which all rational beings must conform and he holds that it cannot be rationally rejected.

He illustrates the force of the imperative with the example of telling a lie. Since lies rely on a background expectation that people normally tell the truth, Kant says that a rational being cannot choose to lie simply when it is convenient or beneficial. This is because if the rule or maxim 'I will lie when it is to my benefit' were to be made universal law – if everybody acted that way – then the general attitude of trust presupposed by the lie would be undermined and the lie itself would be rendered ineffective. In this way, Kant proposes that the only rationally and morally acceptable acts are those which do not treat one's own situation, needs, or desires as special or privileged above those of others, for we are all rational beings worthy of equal dignity and respect as such. In Kant's own words:

> If we attend to what happens in us when we act against duty, we find that we don't (because we *can't*) actually will that our maxim should become a universal law. Rather

we are willing that the opposite of the maxim on which
we are acting should remain as law generally, but we take
the liberty of catering to our preferences by making an
exception – 'just for me, just this once!' (Kant, 1785: 26).

On this basis we contend that there are compelling reasons in
the Kantian view to reject patterns of consumption common in
the Western world (and increasingly elsewhere) in favour of a
lifestyle of relative material simplicity. Right now an expanding
consumer class of more than one billion people is consuming
Earth's resources in a manner that is unprecedented and
entirely exceptional. With the ecological future of the planet
already being jeopardised by current rates of consumption,
it would be utterly catastrophic from an environmental
perspective if such practices were universalised to all 7.4 billion
human beings, to say nothing of the 10 or 11 billion expected
by 2100 (Gerland *et al.*, 2014). From a Kantian perspective,
then, it seems consumer lifestyles as they exist today in wealthy,
technologically developed nations are being pursued in a moral
and rational vacuum, consisting as they do of numerous daily
decisions which treat those making them as exceptions to the
rules of reason and equality under the moral law.

Yet Kant understood that, despite being capable of rational
deliberation and choice, our wills regularly come under the
influence of motivations which do not always find accord with
our reason: we do not always do the right thing simply because
it is the right thing. The fact is, Kant says, human beings cultivate and fall prey to their own personal preferences which
impede the free action of their rational wills; if it were not so, he
claims, a perfectly rational will would never feel constrained by
its moral duty. Unfortunately for the Kantian, humans are far
from being perfect moral agents, but this in no way provides us
an excuse for ignoring our duty. Even with the perhaps enticing
prospect of that new car, big house, or even phone upgrade
or cup of coffee, from the Kantian perspective we are all still
bound by the categorical responsibility to live in a way which
is sustainable and universalisable, and which considers the

whole of humanity both now and in the future. For Kant, blindly following the standard practice of our friends, neighbours, or society at large is no justification at all.

5. Virtue Ethics and Voluntary Simplicity

So far we have discussed how some relatively modern ethical and moral positions may warrant decreased material consumption, yet some of the oldest and most influential advocates of the relationship between the good life and material simplicity come from the ancient Greek philosophers who, despite deep disagreement on various matters, found considerable accord in their praise and practice of simple living. Perhaps this should be no surprise, given the natural overlap of simplicity with the traditional virtues of temperance, frugality, prudence, and self-control. However, the case for material simplicity as a virtue in its own right has not often been stated by philosophers. In this section, following the work of Cafaro and Gambrel (2009), we will briefly outline and discuss the possible place of voluntary simplicity within a virtue ethics framework that dates back to the ancient Greeks. Voluntary simplicity should become a more prominent part, we suggest, of the resurgence in virtue ethics that has occurred in the last generation or so.

Broadly defined, the virtues are those qualities which, to the extent they are present in any given person, society, or institution, make that person, society, or institution a good one: traits on which depend the present and future flourishing of those immediately concerned, as well as that of all others worthy of consideration. The ancient Greeks held that possession of the virtues led to *eudaimonia*; an essential component in a good life but notoriously difficult to translate, perhaps being best approximated as 'flourishing' or 'true happiness'. Naturally, any account of the virtues will thus be determined in large part by the form one believes the good life to take and in what true happiness and flourishing are thought to consist. Yet *eudaimonia* as conceived by the Greeks is not a subjective self-assessment or merely the personal sense of happiness, for even if one thinks oneself to be happy, *eudaimonia* is impossible wherever the virtues are lacking or have been misidentified. The genuine virtues are only those which in fact do lead to *eudaimonia* in its true form, and which are applicable and relevant to all human lives, irrespective of place or time.

Furthermore, the virtuous person acts out of motivation from the virtues, rather than only as a means to some other end. As a result, even many honest actions do not make a person honest, for he or she may be acting honestly only in order to garner a good reputation or to avoid the consequences of being caught in lies. Additionally, the truly virtuous person knows how and when to act, and knows what kind of action is called for by the virtues in a given situation. Such a person has *phronesis*, or practical wisdom; the ability to properly discern what is right rather than act in obedience to immature or simplistic notions of virtue. The honest person tells the truth, but with *phronesis* knows when tact is in order. In the same way, without *phronesis*, the generous person may not know what to gift or when to stop giving. The wisdom to see the big picture as well as the critical details of specific circumstances is therefore indispensable to the understanding and practice of real virtue.

Within this approach, we hold that simplicity may rightly be considered one of the virtues, essentially agreeing with Cafaro and Gambrel (2009: 90) in defining it as 'the virtue disposing us to act appropriately within the sphere of our consumer decisions', whether these decisions are large or small, one-off or repeated. Understood this way, simplicity helps us see clearly what we need to flourish and be happy when it comes for instance to things we purchase and acquire, and also identify which things are ultimately irrelevant to *eudaimonia* or how those things, if pursued, may diminish or hinder it in our lives. Additionally, simplicity would include the wisdom to understand where and how our personal decisions will impact the happiness and flourishing of others, making us more able to perceive the kind of society and world to which various decisions would lead.

Accordingly, the virtue of simplicity implies regular,

thoughtful introspection and reflection, leading to more conscious consumption in line with a deeper understanding of what is truly valuable and important in life. As such, we suggest that the earnest practice of simplicity will typically result in significantly decreased and alternate forms of consumption when compared to the average in the most developed countries. It is also worth noting that while over-consumers in these nations are the clear focus for the present discussion, simplicity likely remains a virtue even for those with very little opportunity to consume material objects, many of whom are quite justified in trying to increase their level of material consumption. While we acknowledge that the moral burden of simplicity falls squarely at the feet of those who have much, we cautiously suggest that those with little (but sufficient) may still benefit from conscious consideration regarding the right material goods to consume, as well as the cultivation of discipline to avoid making unwise decisions in this sphere.

But can simplicity rightly be called a virtue? That is, does the ability to make wise and appropriate consumer decisions promote and help maintain individual, societal, and planetary flourishing? First of all, we suggest that the wise and virtuous person will see that the planet's ecological systems are already strained, especially by the consumption practices of roughly the richest 1.5 billion of its inhabitants, and that the continuation and extension of such practices risks ecosystemic collapse, thereby endangering the lives and wellbeing of the millions or even billions most vulnerable to environmental change (Gardiner, 2011). In the face of this reality, it is relatively simple to see how careful moderation of consumption and the ability to make informed and appropriate consumer decisions directly impacts human (and non-human) flourishing on a global scale.

Yet despite the pressing environmental need to moderate consumption, many see this limitation as antithetical to personal happiness and good living. Does virtue simply demand that we sacrifice our own pleasure for the good of the planet and the human race as a whole? Fortunately, it does not seem that this is so. As noted earlier, a growing body of work is emerging which suggests that by de-emphasising material things, we stand to gain in diverse and often profound ways in the non-material aspects of our lives. By resisting the consumerist impulses to needlessly upgrade and acquire, many of us can save ourselves from financial stress due to over-commitment and debt, while simultaneously freeing up time and money we can spend on non-material pleasures such as time with friends and family, as well as in pursuit of personal passions, projects, and goals. In a wider social context, this time and money can also be directed into volunteer and community groups, making it easier and more enjoyable for us to develop and express other virtues including generosity, compassion, and kindness. Deeper community involvement also affords us the opportunity to form and strengthen bonds across social boundaries, minimising tensions and curtailing a host of social ills. Furthermore, even affluent societies depend fundamentally upon basic ecosystem services that are being eroded by overconsumption; simplicity helps to maintain and protect these and in so doing allows for flourishing societies into the future. In many ways then, irrespective of the modern environmental crises facing us, simplicity remains a virtue as it serves to maintain and promote a balanced positive personal and social outlook while fostering other, overlapping virtues and cultivating fertile ground for the growth of others.

Finally, even with these strengths, it is commonly objected that since a healthy economy is essential for a flourishing society, simplicity should be opposed on the grounds that it threatens economic growth. Unfortunately, a proper response to this important objection cannot be offered here, so it must suffice for us simply to echo Cafaro and Gambrel in their conviction that 'the endless growth economy is an ecological impossibility and a blind alley in the human career' (2009: 105). Perhaps the first step to a better world involves learning to appreciate the virtue of voluntarily moderating our consumption as we choose to live out the fact that true happiness will never come from the things we can buy. Genuine flourishing lies beyond consumer culture.

6. Christianity and Voluntary Simplicity

Throughout history, many diverse religious and spiritual traditions have defended simple living in some form, eschewing materialism and cautioning against greed. This remarkable consensus is likely due, in part, to the realisation that the more time and energy one dedicates to materialistic pursuits, the less one has to devote to the non-material aspects of life, including the spiritual dimension.

However, the consumer cultures of the modern world first appeared and remain strongest in nations with a dominant Christian heritage, and even among the more than two billion people worldwide professing Christian faith, many live in countries with the greatest material affluence and consumption. Therefore, while various religious and spiritual traditions can and do mount forceful arguments for simple living, among these the Christian case for voluntary simplicity and against materialism likely holds the strongest pull for much of consumer society today, due to its cultural influence in the West, and it is for these reasons it receives in-depth treatment here. The discussion that follows focuses on the biblical grounds for material simplicity and rejecting the consumerist craving for money and things. Unsurprisingly, however, many prominent Christian thinkers including St Francis, Aquinas, Calvin, Wesley and, most recently, Pope Francis, have put forward critiques of unnecessary consumption, especially where it causes or contributes to spiritual, social, and environmental ills.

A core element of the Christian message is the recognition that human lives are mis-oriented; that our hearts and minds are regularly not set on the things they should be, and our attentions too easily wander from the good things which truly enrich us, deeply nurture us, and for which we are intended to live. As such, the call for a radical reorientation of one's life was fundamental to Jesus' ministry and is clearly evident in the gospel accounts from his early public teaching onwards, his first words recorded in the Gospel of Mark commending the people of Galilee to 'Repent and believe the good news!' (Mark 1:15).[1] To 'repent' means to change one's mind or purpose; to think differently than before, or to turn away from one thing and towards another. What would Jesus have us turn away from? Anything that distracts us from following him or which keeps us from living our lives according to the good purposes God intends for us.

Thus the 'good news' Jesus preached is that God has promised that all who trust in him will 'have life, and have it to the full.' (John 10:10). For Jesus, as well as the biblical authors, even placing too great an emphasis on things that are not inherently bad can lead to unhealthy obsession which causes God to become increasingly ignored and our conduct to falter. For example, the desire to see one's children make wise decisions, if not balanced, can easily morph into overbearing parenting, or the desire to be agreeable, if unchecked, can lead to cowardice in the face of conflict with majority opinion (Colossians 3:21, Exodus 23:2).

However, one of the primary dangers Christians are exhorted time and again to guard themselves against is the love of money and material affluence, lest it fatally distract from appropriate love of God. Yet it should be made clear that this is not because money or material objects themselves are evil; indeed, these things are given by God for good and ultimately belong to him (see, e.g., Gen. 1, Deut. 10:14, Psalm 89:11, Psalm 24:1, Job 41:11, Heb. 2:10). Thus, humans are stewards rather than outright owners of all material wealth, and are therefore expected to think and act accordingly.

Millennia before modern-day consumer culture the biblical authors seamlessly brought together deep theological truth and commonsense wisdom in their advice and warnings regarding the desire for wealth. The apostle Paul – while imprisoned for his faith – writes to the church in Philippi that contentedness with one's situation does not ultimately come from material circumstance, but from an attitude of thankfulness for all that

---

1. All biblical references are from the New International Version (NIV), Holy Bible.

one has, material and immaterial, 'whether well fed or hungry, whether living in plenty or in want' (Phil. 4:12). Such an attitude refuses to look jealously to others who have more than we do and shuns the grasping desire always to want more than we have, for it acknowledges that our lives are not ultimately founded upon material things.

As the writer to the Hebrews puts it, 'Keep your lives free from the love of money and be content with what you have. For God has said, "Never will I leave you; never will I forsake you"' (Heb. 13:5). This approach comes into pointed conflict with the increasingly popular message of 'prosperity theology' which casts the godly life as a means to material abundance, an outlook which is antithetical to scripture and the mission of Christ. Moreover, Paul laments in his letter to Timothy, a church leader in Ephesus, that 'Some people, eager for money, have wandered from the faith and pierced themselves with many griefs', leading not only to spiritual affliction, but apparently outward troubles as well (1 Tim. 6:10). In this way, focusing heavily on material things diverts our attention from the non-material dimension of being, which we neglect to our own harm.

Similarly, much of the wisdom literature of the Old Testament stresses the folly of prioritising wealth and material gain too highly, cautioning 'not [to] wear yourself out to get rich; have the wisdom to show restraint' (Prov. 23:4). Instead, the wise favour the path of sufficiency: 'give me neither poverty nor riches, but give me only my daily bread' (Prov. 30:8), for anything else can easily lead to the dishonour of God. The Teacher in the book of Ecclesiastes observes that 'Whoever loves money never has enough; whoever loves wealth is never satisfied with his income' (Ecc. 5:10), but rather lives life on an ever-dissatisfying hedonic treadmill. This Teacher identifies himself as king in Jerusalem, detailing his life of conspicuous consumption in which he denied himself nothing his eyes desired, yet he reflects that 'when I surveyed all that my hands had done and what I had toiled to achieve, everything was meaningless, a chasing after the wind' (Ecc. 2:11). He elaborates further, remarking upon the simple but powerful truth that no matter how wealthy you become, you cannot take it with you when you depart this life, for a man 'takes nothing from his labour that he can carry in his hand' (Ecc. 5:15), therefore why fixate on needless gain?

However, nowhere is the conflict between love of God and love of money put in more stark terms than by Jesus, who gave uncompromising warnings that 'where your treasure is, there your heart will be also', and 'No one can serve two masters... You cannot serve both God and money' (Matt. 6:21-24). Jesus knows that there are many things vying for the place of God in our lives; that we can come to idolise money and make it our new god. Jesus recognises that if our ultimate goal and greatest love is the acquisition and maintenance of material abundance, from which we hope to derive our security, sense of worth, freedom, the esteem of others, or anything else, we cannot at the same time look to derive them from God. Jesus' strongest language is reserved for such things, for he is in no doubt of the allure and the promise of satisfaction that material objects hold for human beings. Yet he is equally sure of their inability to ultimately satisfy the deep desires of our hearts, saying, 'Watch out! Be on your guard against all kinds of greed; life does not consist in an abundance of possessions' (Luke 12:15). For the Christian, then – and arguably for the spiritual seeker more generally – a life measured by the things you possess is a life disastrously disoriented, for even if you have much, it cannot provide the sense of meaning and purpose most of us seek.

Yet Christians are not only powerfully urged against living for the present material world at the risk of their souls (Matt. 16:26), but this kind of covetous desire also comes into direct conflict with the constant biblical exhortation towards generosity, kindness, and mercy, especially towards the most needy and afflicted (see, e.g., Lev. 19:9-10, Deut. 15:7-11, Psalm 10:17-18, Prov. 14:31, Isaiah 1:17, Micah 6:8, 2 Cor. 9:7, Phil. 2:1-4, Heb. 13:16, 1 John 3:17-18). A full discussion of the profound conflict between unbridled consumerism and Christian social justice is beyond the scope of this chapter. Yet with billions of people in material need in the world today, as well as hundreds of millions more predicted to become so due to the effects of continued environmental degradation, a compelling Christian case can be made that to neglect the present and future suffering of so many, as well as to actively contribute to the circumstances which create and exacerbate this suffering through excessive material consumption, is both thoroughly unbiblical and in opposition to the heart of God.

7. Foucault's Ethics and Voluntary Simplicity

We will now conclude our philosophical evaluation of voluntary simplicity by exploring whether, or to what extent, Michel Foucault's work on ethics may also support or enrich this suffi-ciency-orientated way of life (see Alexander, 2015b). At first this may seem like a tangent but it should become clear that Foucault's ethical position can be fairly described as a post-structuralist reinterpretation of virtue ethics, and indeed Foucault regularly and openly acknowledges his debts to the ancient Greeks, especially the Cynics and the Stoics (see Foucault, 1985). As we hope to show, examining voluntary simplicity through this post-structuralist lens can offer important new insights into the complexities of moral and ethical thinking and practice. At the same time, even more than previous sections, we accept that the brevity of the following analysis may raise more questions than it answers, but we trust that those questions will nevertheless enrich the discussion if only by problematising it.

We will begin by outlining in the most general terms the impli-cations Foucault's post-structuralism has on moral philosophy. His critique arises out of a deep scepticism about the very search for universal or objective moral truths that are applicable to all people, in all places, irrespective of context. As Foucault and the broader school of post-structuralists, neo-pragmatists, and deconstructionists argue, truth, including moral truth, must be expressed in language, and since language is a human creation, so must truth, ultimately, be a human creation. Furthermore, since language is inherently shifting and unstable and always subject to various interpretive ambiguities, there will never be one and only one moral code that is true for all people in all places, times, and circumstances. For even if we knew which moral code was the one and only one to obey – the Ten Commandments, for example, or Bentham's 'greatest happiness principle' – its context-dependent application would inevitably require interpretation, and interpretation is always a function of one or other paradigm of understanding and not an objective reflection of a pre-existing and eternal metaphysical reality.

But what becomes of moral discourse if the search for a universal moral code is given up? This is the question Foucault put his mind to in his books and essays that make up his so-called 'ethical turn'. It is in these texts where Foucault develops his notion of ethics as 'an aesthetics of existence' (Foucault, 1985; Foucault, 2000), which he presents as an alternative mode of ethical practice that can be taken up, by default, one might say, in the absence of a knowable and universalisable morality.

Foucault's strategy is to problematise the notion of 'selfhood' by arguing that the 'self', far from being as independent and autonomous as philosophers such as Kant have typically supposed, is in fact inextricably shaped by linguistic and contextual forces, such that *who we are* as individuals is not the determinate product of free decisions made by some autonomous agent, but is instead the product of social and linguistic forces that are largely beyond our control. Foucault does not deny or exclude the possibility of human freedom, however, as some might infer from his early work. Foucault does insist that our identities are socially constructed entities and that we lack a transcendental or purely rational 'self', but he nevertheless carves out a certain, albeit limited, degree of space within which our socially constructed identities *can act upon themselves* for the purpose of 'self-fashioning'. We may not get to choose the raw material of which our identities are constituted, but it nevertheless lies within our power to shape that raw material in various ways, just as the sculptor may make various things from a given lump of clay (a metaphor Foucault borrowed from the Greek Stoics).

According to Foucault, this relationship of the self to the self is the terrain of ethics, and when engaging the age-old ethical question, 'How am I to live?', Foucault suggests that we avoid the traditional search for a moral code and instead ask ourselves (as recommended by the virtue ethicists): 'What type of person should I become?'. Using aesthetic metaphors to describe and develop this process of self-fashioning, Foucault (2000: 262) summarises his ethics by arguing that 'we have to create ourselves as a work of art.'

To be clear, Foucault here is not so much arguing that we should aspire to be beautiful in any cosmetic sense; rather, he is seeking to highlight the fact that, in the absence of a knowable moral code that guides or constrains our actions, we must accept the unavoidable creative or aesthetic burden of shaping ourselves and our actions through deliberate practices or technologies of the self.

How, then, is this relevant to our discussion of voluntary simplicity? To begin with, it can be argued the social and institutional celebration of consumer lifestyles within the most developed societies has been internalised to some extent, socially constructing our identities and our worldviews, often in subtle ways. If it is also the case, however, that our cultures and structures of overconsumption are driving several of the world's most pressing problems – both social and environmental – then it may be that ethical activity today requires that we engage the self by the self for the purpose of *refusing who are* – so far as we are uncritical consumers – and creating new, post-consumerist forms of subjectivity. In other words, ethical practice arguably calls for a rethinking of our assumptions, attitudes, and practices concerning consumption, and this might involve a deliberate reshaping of the self by the self for the purpose of making someone new.

Although the question of 'how one ought to live' is timeless, answering that question inevitably takes place relative to one's own time and circumstances, relative to one's own place in history. Let this acknowledgement of our deep and inescapable historicity provide this chapter with its closing theme. Humans are both creatures and creators of their time. As creatures, many of us have been shaped, in many ways, to varying degrees, into uncritical, high-impact consumers. But as creators, our future (including our future 'self') is always and already opening up, challenging us to confront the question: what type of person should I become? It is hoped that some people might find value in exploring the notion of 'voluntary simplicity as an aesthetics of existence' (Alexander, 2015b), although in Foucauldian spirit, we acknowledge that this need not provide answers to all readers or complete answers to anyone.

8. Conclusion

This chapter has reviewed a range of moral and ethical perspectives and attempted to assess, in a preliminary way, the extent to which those perspectives lend support for the sufficiency-orientated consumption practices of voluntary simplicity. We are the first to admit that we have not provided a comprehensive or 'knock down' philosophical case for voluntary simplicity and recognise that each perspective we reviewed could justify and arguably deserves a paper-length, if not a book-length, treatment. Furthermore, in an age where varieties of post-structuralism or post-modernism retain prominence in philosophical circles, we acknowledge that all our arguments are prone – as all arguments are prone – to deconstruction. Certainly, much more could be said both in defence and criticism of the perspectives reviewed.

Nevertheless, we maintain that a very plausible moral and ethical case has been made for voluntary simplicity, from the range of perspectives reviewed. This suggests, without proving, that there is something of moral and ethical significance to this way of life that is not sufficiently recognised in theory or practice. To the extent that we are correct, the main practical implication is that voluntary simplicity should take a more central place in our moral and ethical education and that the casual acceptance of consumer cultures should be more explicitly and regularly challenged. This may be particularly confronting for those of us in affluent societies, whose lifestyles are being called into question. Nevertheless, we hope that this chapter provokes a broader discussion about the moral and ethical weight of voluntary simplicity, especially in an age of consumer malaise, gross inequality, and ever-deepening environmental crises. Just perhaps voluntary simplicity provides part of a necessary but elegant response to those overlapping challenges.

References

Alexander, S. (ed.). 2009. *Voluntary simplicity: The poetic alternative to consumer culture*, Stead & Daughters, Whanganui.

Alexander, S. 2013. 'Voluntary simplicity and the social reconstruction of law: Degrowth from the grassroots up', *Environmental Values* 22, pp 287–308.

Alexander, S. 2015a. *Prosperous descent: Crisis as opportunity in an age of limits*, Simplicity Institute, Melbourne.

Alexander, S. 2015b. 'Voluntary simplicity as an aesthetics of existence: The art of ethics in a consumer age' in Alexander, S. 2015. *Prosperous descent: Crisis as opportunity in an age of limits*, Simplicity Institute, Melbourne, pp 253–291.

Alexander, S. and McLeod, A. (eds). 2014. *Simple living in history: Pioneers of the deep future*, Simplicity Institute, Melbourne.

Alexander, S. and Ussher, S. 2012. 'The voluntary simplicity movement: A multi-national survey analysis in theoretical context', *Journal of Consumer Culture* 12(1), pp 66–88.

Barnett, C., Cafaro, P., and Newholm, T. 2005. 'Philosophy and ethical consumption' in Harrison, R., Newholm, T., and Shaw, D. (eds). *The Ethical Consumer*, Sage, London, pp 11–24.

Bentham, J. 2007 [1789]. *Introduction to principles of morals and legislation*, Dover, New York.

Burch, M. 2013. *The hidden door: Mindful sufficiency as an alternative to extinction*, Simplicity Institute, Melbourne.

Cafaro, P. 2009. 'Less is more' in Alexander, S. (ed.). 2009. *Voluntary simplicity: The poetic alternative to consumer culture*, Stead & Daughters, Whanganui, pp 127–133.

Cafaro, P., and Gambrel, J. 2009. 'The virtue of simplicity', *Journal of Agricultural and Environmental Ethics* 23(1), p. 85.

Diener, E., Helliwell, J., and Kahneman, D. 2010. *International differences in well-being*, Oxford University Press, Oxford.

Diener, E. and Seligman, M. 2004. 'Beyond money: Toward an economy of well-being', *Psychological Science in the Public Interest* 5, 1–31.

Easterlin, R. 1995. 'Will raising the incomes of all increase the happiness of all?', *Journal of Economic Behavior & Organization* 27, pp 35–47.

Easterlin, R. 2013. *Happiness and economic growth: The evidence*, Discussion Paper No. 7187, January 2013, pp 1–30.

Elgin, D. 1998 (revised edn). *Voluntary simplicity: Toward a way of life that is outwardly simple, inwardly rich*, William Morrow, New York.

Foucault, M. 1985. *The uses of pleasure: The history of sexuality* Vol 2, Random House, New York.

Foucault, M. 2000. 'On the genealogy of ethics', in Michel Foucault, *Ethics: Essential works* Vol. I, Penguin, London.

Gardiner, S. 2011. *The perfect moral storm: The ethical tragedy of climate change*, Oxford University Press, Oxford.

Gerland, P., Raftery, A., Sevcikova, H., *et al.* 2014. 'World population stabilization unlikely this century', *Science* 346(6206), pp 234–7.

Gregg, R. 2009 [1936]. 'The value of voluntary simplicity' in Alexander, S. (ed.). *Voluntary simplicity: The poetic alternative to consumer culture*, Stead & Daughters, Whanganui, pp 111–126.

Hamilton, C. 2003. *Growth fetish*, Allen & Unwin, Crows Nest.

Hamilton, C. and Denniss, R. 2005. *Affluenza: When too much is never enough*, Allen & Unwin, Crows Nest.

New International Version (NIV), Holy Bible (1984 and 2011 translations), Zondervan, Grant Rapids.

Intergovernmental Panel on Climate Change (IPCC). 2013. 'Climate Change 2013: The Physical Science Basis (Fifth Assessment Report)'.

Kahneman, D. and Deaton, A. 2010. 'High income improves evaluation of life but not emotional well-being', PNSA 107(38), pp 16489–16493.

Kant, I. 1785. *Groundwork for the metaphysics of morals*, available at: www.earlymoderntexts.com (accessed 16 December 2016).

Kasser, T. 2002. *The high price of materialism*, MIT Press, Cambridge.

Lane, R. 2000. *The loss of happiness in market democracies*, Yale University Press, New Haven.

Latouche, S. 2014. 'Essays on frugal abundance', Simplicity Institute Reports, available at: http://simplicityinstitute.org/publications (accessed 20 December 2016).

Layard, R. 2005. *Happiness: Lessons from a new science*, Penguin Press, New York.

Layard, R. *et al.* 2010. 'Does relative income matter? Are the critics right?' In Diener, E., Helliwell, J., and Kahneman, D. (eds). *International differences in well-being*, Oxford University Press, Oxford, New York.

MacAskill, W. 2016. *Doing good better: How effective altruism can help you help others, do work that matters, and make smarter choices about giving back*, Avery, New York.

Meadows, D., Randers, J., and Meadows, D. 2004. *Limits to growth: The 30-year update*, Chelsea Green Publishing, White River Junction, Vt.

Mill, J.S. 2012 [1863]. *Utilitarianism*, Renaissance Classics, Nelson.

Princen, T. 2005. *The logic of sufficiency*, MIT Press, Cambridge.

Purdey, S. 2010. *Economic growth, the environment, and international relations: The growth paradigm*, Routledge, New York.

Ripple, W. *et al.* 2016. 'Bushmeat hunting and extinction risk to the world's mammals', *Royal Society Open Science* (19 October 2016), DOI: 10.1098/rsos.160498.

Shi, D. 2007 (revised edn). *The simple life: Plain living and high thinking in American culture*, University of Georgia Press, Athens.

Singer, P. 1972. 'Famine, affluence, and morality' in Sher, G. (ed.). 1996. *Moral philosophy: Selected readings* (2nd edn), Harcourt Brace College Publishers, Fort Worth, pp 694–704.

Singer, P. 2009. *Animal liberation: The definitive classic of the animal movement*, HarperCollins, New York.

Soper, K. 2008. 'Alternative hedonism, cultural theory and the role of aesthetic revisioning', *Cultural Studies* 22(5), p. 567.

Steffan, W. *et al.* 2015. 'Planetary boundaries: Guiding human development on a changing planet', *Science* 347(6223), DOI: 10.1126/science.1259855.

Trainer, T. 2010. *The transition to a sustainable and just world*, Envirobook, Sydney.

Vanenbroeck, G. (ed.) 1991. *Less is more: An anthology of ancient and modern voices raised in praise of simplicity*, Inner Traditions, Vermont.

WWF, 2016. *Living planet report 2016*, available at: http://www.worldwildlife.org/pages/living-planet-report-2016 (accessed 16 December 2016).

3

PERMACULTURE AND TRANSITION TOWNS: URBAN RENEWAL 'FROM BELOW'

1. Introduction*

Theories of urban development typically look to governments, local and national, to take the lead in transforming urban landscapes to promote sustainability and wellbeing. This is especially so when the problems requiring a coordinated response – such as climate change – are deep, urgent, and often 'wicked'. Nevertheless, in many parts of the world today, including Australia, recent and current government policies provide little hope that the range of structural changes necessary to create more sustainable, low-carbon cities will emerge from the 'top down'. Despite paying lip service to sustainability issues, most political actors still operate firmly within an out-dated growth paradigm where new roads, new coal mines, or fracking for oil and gas are touted as solutions to urban transport and energy problems, and too often we see cities continuing to eat away at their surrounding greenways with conventional, sprawling, poorly designed housing developments. Business-as-usual more or less prevails.

So far as governments are failing us, it becomes ever more important to look toward 'niche' grassroots movements as the

---

* This chapter was co-authored by Samuel Alexander and Jonathan Rutherford.

key to urban renewal 'from below' (Seyfang and Haxeltine, 2012; Smith, 2007). In the socio-technical transitions literature (e.g., Kemp, Schot, and Hoogma, 1998) the term niche often refers to a 'protected space' that a government provides to a promising social, economic, or technological innovation that has the potential to refine or even replace an incumbent system or 'regime' (Geels, 2002). But a niche can also refer to innovative activities or practices that lie outside and yet challenge a regime, without being a space protected by the state, as such. Marc Wolfram (2017) argues that cities themselves provide protected spaces in the sense that individuals and communities are able to articulate and enact diverse 'alternative ontologies' and 'spatial imaginaries' of socio-technical change (Longhurst, 2015) because cities fundamentally enable the manifestation of diversity. Furthermore, Gill Seyfang and Adrian Smith (2007: 585) use the term niche to include grassroots initiatives, which they define as 'networks of activists and organizations generating novel bottom-up solutions for sustainable development'. These networks may challenge a regime even if governmental protection or assistance is not provided. Grassroots innovations within urban contexts provide a range of niches that Wolfram (2017) notes have gone 'largely unexplored' within the sustainability transitions literature.

This chapter provides an analysis of one such niche – the emerging Transition Towns Movement (hereafter TTM), which provides one of the more well-known social movements to develop during the last decade in response to overlapping energy, environmental, and economic crises (Hopkins, 2009; Hopkins, 2011; Aiken, 2012; Barry and Quilley, 2008; North and Cato, 2012). Whereas the more established Ecovillage Movement has generally sought to escape the urban context to establish experiments in alternative living, the TTM, motivated by similar concerns, tends to accept the challenge of transforming urban life from *within* the urban boundary. As argued in this chapter, this grassroots movement has relevance to urban transitions, generally (Taylor, 2012; Pelling and Navarrete, 2011) and Australian urban development, in particular, due to the sprawling, suburban nature of most Australian cities and the uninspired state of Australian politics (Bay, 2013; Holmgren, 2012; Mason and Whitehead, 2012). In the absence of progressive political leadership, might the TTM niche (see Seyfang and Haxeltine, 2012) or something like it need to play a role creating new urban landscapes? What potential has this movement for changing the regime? What are the challenges it might face? And could cities ever become interconnected hubs of Transition Towns at large?

Since its inception in 2005, the TTM has spread to many countries around the world, including Australia, and is gaining increased attention from academics, politicians, and media (Feola and Nunes, 2014). Its fundamental aims are to respond to the overlapping challenges of climate change, peak oil, social isolation, and economic instability by decarbonising and relocalising the economy through a community-led model of change based on permaculture design principles (Holmgren, 2002). Rather than waiting for governments to lead, communities in this movement are embracing the 'power of just doing stuff' (Hopkins, 2013), getting active trying to build the new world within the shell of the old. In doing so, the movement runs counter to the dominant narrative of globalisation, techno-optimism, and economic growth, and instead offers a positive, participatory, highly localised but more humble vision of a low-carbon future, as well as an evolving roadmap for getting there through grassroots activism (Wilson, 2012). In the words of Tim Jackson, this international movement is 'the most vital social experiment of our time' (see Hopkins, 2011; see also, Broto and Bulkeley, 2013).

Recently, Australian permaculture theorist and educator David Holmgren – whose work has significantly shaped the TTM in theory and practice – has called for grassroots movements, such as the TTM, to 'retrofit the suburbs' (Holmgren 2012). Such a process would involve individuals and communities acting locally – with or without government support – to try to radically transform their urban landscapes by thinking creatively about how to make the best of an infrastructure that is often poorly design from social and environmental perspectives.

Defining activities include attempts to localise food production and connect with local farmers; increase home-based economies; relearn the skills of self-sufficiency; practise frugality and voluntary simplicity to reduce consumption; organise sharing and barter schemes beyond the formal economy; take the energy efficiency of their homes and lifestyles into their own hands; as well as attempt to decarbonise energy use not only through household and community-based renewable energy systems but also by minimising energy consumption through behaviour change (e.g., cycling more and driving less). If this movement evolved from niche activity to mainstream consciousness, how far could it transform the urban landscape in Australia and elsewhere? And what challenges should it expect from the existing regime if it really began to scale up?

This chapter will explore these issues, focusing on the promise and challenges of urban and suburban transformation 'from below'. In applying transitions theory, we acknowledge that the precise delineation of niche and regime cannot always be sharply defined, and the TTM movement raises special challenges here. Following Seyfang and Haxeltine (2012: 386), we maintain flexibility in our use of regime, recognising that participants in the TTM act across and within various socio-technical regimes (transport, food, energy, housing, etc.) while at the same time being focused on a 'broad societal transition' away from a regime of fossil-fuel dependency, growth, and globalisation. The analysis begins, therefore, by outlining that broad societal regime, which provides the necessary context for understanding the TTM's goals of resilience and relocalisation. After providing that groundwork, the chapter sketches a vision of what urban life might look like if the TTM scaled up in response to deepening crisis in the regime, and concludes by considering some obstacles that lie in the way of such a transition.

2. The Regime of Growth and Globalisation

Any theory of 'transition' needs to have both a robust understanding of the current state of things as well as some conception (even if it is constantly evolving) of the goal or ideal state that would represent a successful transition. Only then would anyone be in a position to coherently consider questions of transition – that is, strategic questions about how to get from where we are to where we would like to be.

We acknowledge that this framing sits uneasily with the approach adopted by most socio-technical transitions scholars (e.g., Rotmans, Kemp, and Asselt, 2001), who have shown a reluctance to describe in advance what a sustainable society might look like. While the literature recognises the importance of beginning with a clear analysis of the existing situation (Loorbach, 2010), caution is understandably shown with regard to future envisioning, because the details of what sustainability implies in practice can never be known in advance. Thus we must constantly adjust our theories of transition accordingly, in the face of ever-changing challenges, risks, and opportunities. Be that as it may, if questions of transition are asked having misunderstood the existing situation, or having misconceived the most appropriate responses to existing problems, then there is a very real risk that one's theory of transition, motivated by the best of intentions, may be applied in ways that fail to effectively produce any positive effect or, worse still, may even be counter-productive to one's cause. After all, if our map is poorly drawn and our compass is broken, we are unlikely to arrive at where we need to go.

In order to understand the TTM, therefore, it is critical to understand the way many of its participants assess the global predicament and what they see as the most coherent forms of social, economic, and political action in light of the overlapping crises of our times. To begin with, this means 'thinking globally' about both justice and sustainability, for only then can one know how best to 'act locally'.

There are now 7.4 billion people on Earth, and recent studies suggest we're heading for more than 9.5 billion by mid-century and 11 billion by 2100 (Gerland *et al.*, 2014). This global population, even if it stopped growing today, is placing tremendous burdens on planetary ecosystems. By all range of indicators (climatic, oceans, deforestation, top soil erosion, resource depletion, biodiversity loss, etc.) the global economy is now in gross ecological overshoot, year by year degrading the biophysical foundations of life in ways that are unsustainable (Steffan, Richardson, Rockstrom *et al.*, 2015). Needless to say, consumption practices in the most developed regions of the world are by far the most environmentally impactful, although the developing world seems to be following (or being forced onto) the same high-impact, fossil-fuel dependent industrial path taken by the most developed nations. Let us not pretend that all the talk about 'sustainable development' in recent decades has produced sustainable development.

Despite the global economy being in this overgrown state of ecological overshoot, we also know that billions of people on the planet are, by any humane standard, under-consuming. If these people are to raise their living standards to some dignified level of material sufficiency, as they have every right to do, it is likely that this will place further burdens on already overburdened ecosystems. All this and more is radically calling into question the legitimacy of the high-impact forms of urban life that have evolved in the most developed regions of the world.

And yet, despite the fact that humanity is making unsustainable demands on a finite biosphere, all nations on the planet (including or especially the richest nations) are seeking to grow their economies without apparent limit. This is highly problematic, to say the least, because of the close connection between economic growth (in terms of GDP) and rising energy and resource consumption (Weidmann *et al.*, 2015). It is all very well to point to the potential of technology and efficiency improvements to produce 'green growth', but the fact is that as the world gets distracted by such theoretical possibilities (Alexander, 2015: Ch. 1), the face of Gaia is vanishing.

Without going further into detail, suffice to say that most in the TTM seem to frame their analysis of the world by this 'limits to growth' perspective (Meadow *et al.*, 2004; Hopkins and Miller, 2012; Turner, 2014). They conclude that globalising the high-consumption, energy-intensive ways of living prevalent in

the developed regions of the world would be ecologically catastrophic, and reject the theory that all nations on the planet can
grow their economies while sufficiently 'decoupling' economic
activity from environmental impact by way of technological
advancement and efficiency improvements. The extent of
decoupling required is far too great (Alexander, 2016). Efficiency
without sufficiency is lost.

The TTM is also generally sceptical about the ability of
renewable energy to easily replace fossil fuels – especially the
94 million barrels of oil that are consumed every day – from
which it follows that the most developed regions of the world
will almost certainly need to adapt to an energy descent future
if 100% renewable energy supply is achieved. But given the
close connection between energy and economic activity (Ayres
and Warr, 2009), reduced energy supply implies that those
developed, energy-intensive societies, such as Australia, will
need to go through a phase of planned economic contraction,
with the aim of leaving sufficient 'ecological room' for the poorest nations to provide a dignified standard of living for those
currently destitute. This will require the rich nations to create
new 'post-growth' or 'degrowth' forms of economy, while at the
cultural level variously reimagining the good life beyond consumer culture (Alexander, 2015). Tinkering around the edges of
growth capitalism will not cut it.

Granted, most people – including most socio-technical
transitions scholars? – are not ready to accept these deep implications of the global situation, but only by understanding and
acknowledging the true extent of the ecological predicament
and the limits of technological and market-based solutions
can one understand why the TTM has emerged in the form it
has. It is important to bear this 'limits to growth' perspective
in mind when evaluating the TTM's vision(s) of urban transformation outlined below, which might otherwise be interpreted
as being too radical. Indeed it is radical in many ways, but this
is defended on the grounds that it is a response proportionate
to the magnitude and urgency of the overlapping crises we face.

3. The Transition Town Niche of Resilience and Localisation

Having outlined, very briefly, the way many in the TTM seem to understand the global predicament, we are now in a position to outline the movement's 'theory of change'. The first point to note here is that if growth economics is the primary cause of the global predicament, then any adequate response to current crises will require transitioning 'beyond growth'. As the Einsteinian dictum goes, we cannot solve today's problems with the same thinking that caused them.[1]

If it is the case, then, that governments are incapable or unwilling to question the growth paradigm – which seems to be a fair description of most governments around the world today, including in Australia – then it follows that governments will shape their activities and policies (including urban development policies) within a growth paradigm that cannot solve the problems they are trying to address. For this reason, the TTM emerged to explore the potential of a grassroots or community-led approach to societal change 'from below'. The TTM movement therefore provides a challenge to the dominant approach within socio-technical transitions literature which primarily looks to technological and market-based solutions to existing crises (see Shove and Walker, 2007). The TTM can be understood to be privileging the *social* over the *technical*, casting doubt on the idea that existing crises can be solved by or within a globalised capitalist economy focused on economic growth.

The rationale for grassroots activity is that 'if we wait for governments, it'll be too late. If we act as individuals, it'll be too little. But if we act as communities, it might be just enough, just in time' (Hopkins, 2013: 45). According to some commentators, this approach represents a 'pragmatic turn' (Barry and Quilley, 2008: 2) insofar as it focuses on *doing* sustainability here and

---

1. This section draws upon Esther Alloun and Samuel Alexander, 'The Transition Town Movement: Questions of Diversity, Power, and Affluence', *Simplicity Institute Report* 14g: 1–25.

now. In other words, it is a form of 'DIY politics' (Barry and Quilley, 2009: 3), one that does not involve waiting for governments to provide solutions but rather depends on an actively engaged citizenry to drive the change at the local level.

The paradigm shift of the TTM is articulated around notions of 'decarbonisation' and 'relocalisation' of production and consumption. What this means in terms of transforming urban landscapes will be unpacked further below, but the basic dynamic is that decarbonisation is necessary and desirable for reasons of climate change and looming peak oil, and given how carbon intensive global trade is, decarbonisation implies relocalising economic processes as far as possible as well as consciously moving away from high-consumption lifestyles toward ways of living informed by an ethics of frugality, moderation, and sufficiency.

As well as decarbonisation and relocalisation, another central goal of the movement is to build community 'resilience', a term which can be broadly defined as the capacity of a community or society to withstand shocks and the ability to adapt after disturbances (Hopkins, 2008: Ch. 3). Notably, within the TTM crisis in the current system is typically presented not as a cause for despair but as a transformational opportunity, a prospective change for the better that should be embraced rather than feared (Hopkins, 2011: 45).

When it comes to applying these broad ideas and concerns in practice, the movement's co-founder, Rob Hopkins (2008), outlines a 12-step roadmap that is intended to help communities start, grow, and run a localised 'transition initiative'. These steps involve setting up a steering group, raising awareness about critical issues, developing visible practical projects, organising activities to 're-skill' the community, and formulating an Energy Descent Action Plan. These steps, it should be noted, are fairly generic and demonstrate that the TTM does not propose 'prescriptive solutions' (Hopkins, 2008: 137) or a 'one size fits all' approach, but rather constitutes an 'open-ended experiment' (Barry, 2012: 114) and a broad rethinking of 'how local economies feed, house, and power themselves' (Hopkins, 2012: 74-75).

As one of its defining and most admirable features, the TTM aspires to lead by 'practical example' (Hopkins, 2011: 73). Hopkins (2011: 146) emphasises that the movement should not be 'just a talking shop' and that 'practical manifestations' of relocalisation and decarbonisation are essential to create momentum. As he notes, 'a transition initiative with dirt under its fingernails will gain credibility' and thereby attract new people (Hopkins, 2011: 146). These projects also offer an opportunity for experiential and social learning, connecting or reconnecting with nature, as well as acquiring new skills. This 'Great Reskilling', as Hopkins (2011: 152–154) calls it, is an essential aspect of resilience building and developing local adaptive capacities.

As a practical matter, food usually appears as an early focal point of transition initiatives, and many initiatives offer training in permaculture and organic gardening, cooking and preserving food (Pinkerton and Hopkins, 2009; Bay, 2013). Collective initiatives are also put together to encourage local food provisioning, with the aim of 'delinking food and fossil fuels' (Heinberg and Bomford, in Hopkins, 2011: 56) and promoting bioregionalism. For example, many transition initiatives try to set up a community garden/allotment or a veggie box scheme, organise an urban farmers' market, as well as organise fruit tree and nut tree planting days, seed banks, and seed swap days. Other transition activities include: establishing local currencies and community-based renewable energy projects; organising carpooling schemes, car-free days, educational films nights, bicycle or sewing workshops and cooperatives, and workshops on energy efficiency in the home and workplace (Hopkins, 2011; 2013). These are small-scale illustrations of the ambitious attempt to build resilience and decarbonise the economy, and ultimately – in the long term – to fundamentally restructure the economy to support relocalisation and better promote social and ecological justice (North, 2010).

The Transition Network was founded in 2006 to 'inspire, encourage, connect, support and train communities' on their 'transition' (see Transition Network, 2016). It reinforces the idea of self-organisation, as its objective is not to centralise decision-making but to connect diverse initiatives in order to share experiences, knowledge, skills, and ideas on best practice. In this sense, the Transition Network can be seen as creating a protected space for its own niche, in the hope of replicating, up-scaling, and translating its practices to broader society (Seyfand and Haxeltine, 2012). As of June 2016, the Transition Network had 1258 initiatives registered in over 43 countries (Transition Network, 2016a; Henfrey and Kenrick, 2015).

In Australia, there are at least 43 transition initiatives (Earthwise Harmony, 2016), so the movement has laid down roots. But it remains small, and a literature search suggests that Australian Transition Towns have yet to have been the subject of scholarly empirical studies.[2] Part of the reason the TTM is so small in Australia could be because the global financial crisis, which deeply impacted most parts of the world economy, more or less passed over the Australian economy. Social movements rarely emerge to transform economies during prosperous times – the social discontent is not there to ignite widespread activism and engagement. Nevertheless, we will argue that there are aspects to the Australian urban landscape that might be particularly suitable for the TTM to flourish, suggesting that this movement deserves attention despite its currently small size.

In any case, an interesting aspect of the TTM in relation to transitions theory is that, while the movement indeed aims to change the regime of growth and globalisation, it is nevertheless resigned to the fact that the regime is almost certainly facing an inevitable descent, no matter what, due to environmental limits to growth and the foreseeable decline of fossil fuels in coming years or decades (Mohr *et al.*, 2015). Thus resilience building in the face of regime breakdown is an important goal to work towards, and the perspective we focus on below. We contend that the TTM movement might only come into its own and scale up when crisis in the regime intensifies and provokes local activism in a way that stable and prosperous (albeit deeply unsustainable)

---

2. But see Feola and Nunes (2014) for an international empirical study, including Australia, but in which the specifically Australian data cannot be isolated from other countries.

times do not. In this way, the TTM arguably inverts the approach of most transitions theory: rather than looking to the regime to support the niche (via 'strategic niche management'), the niche of the TTM is actually an attempt to strategically manage the foreseeable deterioration of the incumbent regime.

4. Retrofitting the Suburbs for an Energy Descent Future

Today, most in the TTM are working on figuring out how to make the best of existing urban infrastructure – a task David Holmgren (2012) refers to as 'retrofitting the suburbs for the energy descent future'. It makes sense to begin the Transition process by improving what already exists rather than seeking to create something entirely new. After all, we are hardly going to knock down the suburbs and build things again from scratch in a 'greener' way.

A key advantage of the retrofitting strategy, as outlined below, lies in the power and responsibility it places in individuals, households, and communities just to get started reinventing their neighbourhoods, without waiting for government action – action which, in any case, may not be forthcoming. Indeed, even if government action were to be forthcoming, it may be utterly misconceived (e.g., more roads! more sprawl!), and ultimately do more harm than good by locking in further path dependency. Furthermore, in crisis situations, governments may not always have the resources to solve local problems, in which case building resilience in advance of potential crises is a sensible task for local communities to undertake.

At the personal level, retrofitting the suburbs might involve, for example, taking in boarders by filling an empty room, to prevent further urban sprawl; putting solar panels on the roof; or retrofitting a poorly insulated house, by putting up thick curtains and sealing gaps in windows and doors to increase energy efficiency and minimise energy consumption. Holmgren (2012) and others in the TTM (Hopkins, 2013) are also advocates of transforming the household into a place of production again – as it was in centuries or even decades gone by – rather than leaving them merely as places of consumption, which they have essentially become in most developed urban contexts today. At the communal level, the retrofitting transition strategy could mean working on establishing projects such as farmers markets, sharing networks, community gardens, food-swap groups, skill share workshops, educational film nights, community energy projects, local currencies, or helping on a local wildlife restoration project. Again, the key aims of this broad strategy would be to decarbonise and relocalise economies as far a possible, while enriching community engagement through collective action.

These Transition activities are currently small in the greater scheme of things and are easily dismissed by critics (with some justification) as of trifling transformative significance. Our immediate task, however, is to consider what this movement might become if 'retrofitting the suburbs' came to be embraced and radicalised, not just by a handful of dedicated and informed social activists, but by large segments of a local community or suburb. As implied above, we contend that the most likely 'spark' for this movement to scale up is a deepening crisis in the global economy, although Seyfang and Haxeltine (2012) also offer suggestions for how the movement could scale up and translate its message in advance of crisis. What is clear is that over the long term, if the TTM is to be of any deep transformative significance, it must go beyond current retrofitting and transition activities (Trainer, 2014) and more fundamentally remake suburbs and towns into highly self-sufficient but interconnected urban villages through collective, grassroots action (Trainer, 2016; Trainer, 2010).

As Hopkins (2011: 72–76) emphasises, 'transitioning' is both an inner and outer process. Change is needed not only in the external physical structures, institutions, and organisations upon which societies rest, but also in our worldviews, norms, attitudes, and values. In recognition of this, the Transition model of change attempts to weave together the power of imagination, visioning, and storytelling, with the practical manifestation of these alternative narratives, through the engagement of the head, the heart, and the hands (Hopkins, 2008).

In that spirit, the following section undertakes a 'visioning' exercise that seeks to provoke reflection on what cities might come to look like if, in response to a regime in crisis, the TTM scaled up and succeeded in transforming the urban landscape. The existing literature often examines successful case studies (Roorda *et al.*, 2014) to help guide thinking and action. The value of more creative visioning exercises, such as the following, reside in their potential to help people break free from dominant development and sustainability narratives and scenarios which, we maintain, almost always assume 'green growth' will provide a smooth transition pathway to sustainability without requiring much in the way of lifestyle change. Our underlying argument is that something like what follows may represent 'life within sustainable limits' far more accurately than those mainstream visions of sustainability.

4.1 A vision of 2030: The urban landscape transformed

Let us, then, jump forward to the year 2030 and imagine what urban life might be like if the TTM – or some confluence of similar movements – managed to scale up and transform urban landscapes as crises within the incumbent regime of growth and globalisation intensify. We focus our thought experiment on a generic Australian suburb of mostly single or double story bungalows on blocks of land mostly a quarter-of-an-acre or smaller. Other contexts would require creative adaptation in different ways but motivated by similar values and concerns.

In this future suburb most residents have dug up their back yards and developed productive and diverse permaculture gardens in collaboration with their neighbours, partly motivated by very uncertain and often challenging economic times. A social ethic of frugal self-sufficiency is now widely accepted and practised, driven by these hard economic times. A post-consumerist attitude to waste has emerged, drawing on the Depression-era slogan: 'use it up, wear it out, make it do, or do without.'

Many fences within the neighbourhoods have been removed, wholly or in part, to establish small urban farms and to increase social interaction. Most backyards also house chickens and/ or ducks for eggs, bees for honey and wax, and a few of the larger blocks keep goats for milk and cheese production. Every backyard has a washing line, so electric dryers have become a thing of the past, and water tanks surround houses and sheds to maximize water collection and minimise the need for mains supply. Water consumption is also minimised through simple greywater systems, as well as conscientious showering and washing of clothes.

Most suburban households no longer use flush-toilets, having moved to composting toilet systems after learning how to create their own systems at community workshops, and this will minimise the need for energy-intensive infrastructure development for sewerage in the future. It is now accepted that a civilised society in an era of water scarcity should not defecate into potable water and should instead close the nutrient cycle by turning human and animal waste into nutrient-rich soil for local food production, especially fruit trees (Jenkins, 2005).

In the front yards and in nature strips, a variety of fruit trees, vines, and berries provide some more of the household's food consumption, although since households are not fully self-sufficient, grains and other food stuffs are purchased from or traded at the vibrant local farmers' markets in the weekend. These markets source their food from the bioregion, minimising 'food miles', building local resilience, and leading to almost completely seasonal diets.

Given that many households no longer rely on a private motor vehicle – relying primarily on bikes and public transport instead – some neighbourhoods have been expanding their gardens and urban farms by creating raised garden beds on under-utilised parking lots and even on the sides of roads. People are expected to consult with their neighbours when expanding their gardens into public space but the expansion of urban agriculture has occurred without explicit council approval. Reminiscent of Havana, in Cuba, the new urban landscape could be well described as a permaculture jungle – an 'edible landscape' crammed with long-lived, largely self-maintaining productive plants, especially on the public spaces, parks, footpaths and the roads that have been dug up. This also reduces the 'urban heat island' effect. Local water catchment systems, such as swales and ponds, allow for maximum retention and use of rainwater.

This culture of urban food production is significant not just because it builds resilience and minimises the need for the imported produce of industrial agriculture, it also connects people with the cycles of nature and their land base in ways that the 'supermarket generations' were not, positively shaping the human psyche in subtle but important ways (see Louv, 2011). The abundance of food grown on public land is considered public property, so no one goes hungry. Given that most people eat low-meat, fresh food diets, and exercise more through gardening and cycling, community health is better than it has ever been. The obesity epidemic seems to be quickly fading away. In this way, not only are urban landscapes transforming in positive ways, but so too are the urbanites that inhabit them, each shaping the other in dialectical ways.

Nevertheless, many people lost their jobs in the Second Great Depression of 2019-2023, which was sparked by the US fracking boom going bust, causing the price of oil to rise to levels that placed contractionary pressure on the global economy that was already stagnating under unsupportable levels of public and private debt. Many households that once had two incomes, now have to get by on one, or even one part-time income. In order to deal with this challenging economic contraction, people are essentially forced to contribute to the 'informal' economy through practices of home production, and co-housing has been on the rise for about a decade. The 'tiny house' movement has emerged as a creative response to eliminate most cases of homelessness.

Garages that used to house cars have been converted into workshops, where people now produce furniture, clothes, alcohol, tools, and other useful products – for themselves or for trade

– as well as provide services like bike, shoe, and tool repairs, or education. The days of consumer affluence are gone for most people, but there is a silver lining to all this: when communities take on more of these essential productive functions they become more resilient and cohesive, and the work is generally more fulfilling because it is often creative and necessary to meet important social needs.

As well as reducing dependence on the formal economy, this thriving local economy also minimises the need for travel to places of work, since many people now work from home or only a short bike ride away. In recent years councils have been put under tremendous social pressure to maximise space available for bike lanes, and this has helped strengthen the shift away from fossil fuel-dependent cars. Increasingly, sections of the suburbs are being declared 'car free'. The emergence of the local economy also means that during the day the suburbs are vibrant, densely populated, and safe centres of economic and cultural activity – and are not emptied from 9am to 6pm as they were in the recent past. The fact that there are now sophisticated and interconnected sharing networks within and between suburbs also reduces people's dependence on the formal, monetary economy and greatly reduces wasteful consumption. The internet remains a useful social tool – keeping global cultural and knowledge transfer alive, facilitating sharing, and widely used for video conferencing to avoid air travel – but it is no longer the centre of social life.

The predominately local economy has also brought with it large social benefits, as neighbours have come to see each other as interconnected parts of highly localised self-provision. After all, which community is richer: the one where everybody owns their own cheap drill in affluent isolation? Or the one where the community is connected via a tool shed where a few high-quality tools are shared amongst the neighbourhood? Given that most households are less affluent than previous eras in monetary and material terms, there is far less discretionary income for paid entertainment, so people now spend their leisure time engaging in low-impact creative activity like music or art, and the new forms of local economy that have arisen also provide many avenues for meaningful and fulfilling self-employment as an artisan, often blurring the boundary between work and leisure.

Energy use, particularly in the form of electricity, is used far more frugally than earlier in the 21st century – motivated by high prices – but sufficient supplies for moderate use come from local solar-thermal, wind turbines, and household solar PV. Many households have biogas digesters in their backyards, providing a modest portion of the energy needed for heating and cooking. Carefully managed woodlots beyond the urban boundary also provide some fuel for heating, and a small amount of corn ethanol is produced to provide some liquid fuel for the most necessary industrial tasks. High energy prices have incentivised greatly reduced energy demand, which obviously reduced the amount of renewable energy infrastructure that was required to meet demand, making the transition more affordable. Things such as cycling, insulating houses, more limited use of heaters and air-conditioners, and localising (and reducing) much production has greatly reduced dependence on fossil fuels and global supply chains. Local forests, farms and animals, provide many necessary resources such as timber, clay, bamboo, leather, wool, oils, medicines, wax, mud, and much else.

Over time the existing housing stock will need to be replaced and built with materials sourced as locally as possible, and designed for long-term durability and to the highest standards of energy efficiency. More people and communities take part in the construction of their own homes to reduce costs and liberate people from oppressive mortgages. To limit the resources required, as well as limit the spaces needed to heat and cool, new houses are much smaller than was typically the case in developed nations in earlier decades of the 21st century, and they are more densely inhabited.

As well as suburban transformation, many people have also been incentivised to leave dense, high-rise urban centres by the prospect of far cheaper land and housing in small towns in rural Australia. Small-town rural Australia is undergoing a revitalisation in ways that resemble the urban transformation, outlined above, that has taken place in many large cities. In fact, the scale of small towns actually makes the transformation just outlined easier to implement and maintain.

The movement away from industrial agriculture has meant that there is a large demand for workers in the increasing number of small organic farms on the urban periphery, and this rural or peri-urban revitalisation is also putting less pressure for the large cities to expand. Given that these self-transformed urban landscapes have proven successful over the last decade or so, *new* urban developments have come to be shaped in their vision, with presumptions of distributed energy systems, urban farms, bike lanes, and local economies now being supported, rather than inhibited, by planning decisions (Sharp, 2014). In this way we can come to understand how bold grassroots social movements can, over time, filter upwards and shape top-down politics (Alexander, 2013).

When reflecting on this future scenario, the main point is that most if not all of what has just been described could be achieved by local communities in a relatively short period of time, with or without government support. Ideally, these changes would be made in advance of deepening crisis in the regime, as existing transition towns are attempting to do, but scaling up seems difficult (Seyfang and Haxeltine, 2012) and unlikely in cultures that have become accustomed to (unsustainable) affluence. Indeed, there is evidence suggesting that the growth of the TTM is slowing (Feola and Him, 2016). Nevertheless, we maintain that the TTM remains relevant because it presents a coherent vision for how communities can adapt positively when – as is quite possible and indeed likely – the incumbent regime of growth and globalisation deteriorates over coming years and decades as it collides evermore with the limits to growth.

5. Limits of the Transition Town Movement

There are huge structural and cultural challenges that lie in the way of this niche scaling up to threaten or replace the existing regime. Below we acknowledge three key challenges.

First, individuals and communities live within structures of constraint – infrastructure, economic, political, cultural, etc. – and those structures shape the ways we live our lives (Sanne, 2002). One key challenge faced by social movements seeking urban transformation 'from below' is that some of the structural changes needed to help encourage low-impact living (new energy systems, public transport, bike lanes, etc.) are, it would seem, best made by governments.

Be that as it may, in a context of slow or stagnant political action, the question of how local communities can do the best they can *within existing structural constraints* is a strategic question that deserves heightened attention. After all, if the TTM movement is correct in diagnosing the 'growth paradigm' as central to the problems humanity faces, then governments entrenched in that paradigm are unlikely to foster and are more likely to inhibit the kinds of 'post-growth' sustainability transitions required.

In this light, the TTM declares with worrying plausibility that 'if we wait for governments to act, it'll be too late' (Hopkins, 2013: 45). So even if one perceives great potential in governments to hasten sustainability transitions, it would be foolish to deny the importance of grassroots drivers of change (Seyfang and Smith, 2007). At the very least, such movements can be seen as creating the cultural conditions necessary for 'top-down' action to take root (Alexander, 2013). After all, bold top-down action is unlikely to emerge unless there is a political culture that demands it.

Second, there are some niches that the regime may love to see scaled up and others the regime would resist. For example, if governments could support some new renewable energy technology in ways that ultimately led to a swift decarbonisation transition, then such a regime-change in energy provision could be welcomed by the incumbent system. But would the existing regime actually want the Transition Town niche to succeed in ways outlined above? Probably not. After all, the existing polit-ico-economic paradigm is shaped by the desire for continuous economic growth, and we have seen that the TTM is founded upon a 'limits to growth' perspective that rejects the possibility and even the desirability of limitless growth. The point is that a growth-orientated regime will not want a post-growth niche to scale up, so the TTM may well find that scaling up gets harder, not easier.

Finally, for present purposes, there is a reality, just noted, which the TTM must face: it is, in the greater scheme of things, very small. Transition Towns arguably get a disproportionate amount of media and scholarly attention because their stories of (limited) success are often uplifting and full of promise. This can give the impression the movement is bigger than it really is. But when one looks into the lived reality of Transition Towns one often learns that most of the initiatives are driven by a very small handful of engaged activists within populations that almost entirely are unengaged with transition activities (Feola and Nunes, 2014).

6. Conclusion

It is often expected that academic studies conclude with some notes of optimism, highlighting paths forward that will solve the problems that have been under examination. We will resist that convention in order to highlight our contribution to the transitions literature. The logic of our analysis has been quite simple: (1) Governments do not seem to be doing much to facilitate sustainability transitions, therefore hope arguably resides in the social sphere, which must drive the movements for change. (2) But, promising social movements like the TTM are struggling to scale up and are likely to continue to struggle due to structural lock-in; (3) Therefore, a plausible future scenario is one in which the incumbent regime is not replaced voluntarily in a planned and orderly manner but is replaced instead through a series of social, economic, and environmental crises as the incumbent regime breaks down.

Instead of exploring how the regime could manage a niche

such as the TTM to avoid such crises, our approach in this chapter was to explore the role the TTM could play in managing a regime that looks destined to deteriorate in coming years and decades (Turner, 2014). So in response to the question 'how might the TTM scale up?' we assumed that it may require a deepening crisis of global capitalism, which could provide the incentive to get active in one's community in a way that life does not yet provide for most people living in affluent societies. If it turns out that the TTM fails to transform the urban landscape according to its ambitious vision, then *trying* to do so now arguably still remains a good use of time, resources, and energy, because this may help build local resilience as the existing regime grows itself into ever-deepening crises.

Without false optimism, then, our challenge in coming years may best be understood as managing as positively as we can a regime destined for decline. We have argued that the TTM or something like it provides a coherent pathway for turning that looming crisis into an opportunity for urban renewal.

References

Aiken, G. 2012. 'Community transitions to low carbon futures in the Transitions Towns Network (TTN)', *Geography Compass* 6(2), pp 89–99.

Alexander, S. 2013. 'The voluntary simplicity movement and the social reconstruction of law: Degrowth from the grassroots up', *Environmental Values* 22(2), pp 287–308.

Alexander, S. 2015. 'Prosperous descent: Crisis as opportunity in an age of limits', Simplicity Institute, Melbourne.

Alexander, S. 2016. 'Policies for a post-growth economy', *MSSI Issues Paper* No. 6, pp 1–15.

Ayres, R., and Warr, B. 2009, *The economic growth engine: How energy and work drive material prosperity*, Edward Elgar, Cheltenham.

Barry, J., Quilley, S. 2008. 'Transition towns: "Survival", "resilience" and sustainable communities – outline of a research agenda', *Advances in Ecopolitics* 2, pp 14–37.

Barry, J., Quilley, S. 2009. 'The transition to sustainability: Transition towns and sustainable communities' in L. Leonard and J. Barry (eds),

Ch. 1. *The transition to sustainable living and practice*, Emerald Group, Bingley.

Barry, J. 2012. *The politics of actually existing unsustainability*, Oxford University Press, Oxford.

Bay, U. 2013. 'Transition town initiatives promoting transformational community change in tackling peak oil and climate change challenges', *Australian Social Work* 66(2), pp 171–186.

Broto, V. and Bulkeley, H. 2013. 'A survey of urban climate change experiments in 100 cities', *Global Environmental Change* 23, pp 92–102.

Earthwise Harmony. 2016. 'Transition Towns Australia'. http://www.earthwiseharmony.com/CONNECT/EH-Transition-Towns-Australia.html (accessed 6 June 2016).

Feola, G. and Him, M.N. 2016. 'The diffusion of the Transition Network in four European countries', *Environment and Planning A* (in press).

Feola, G., and Nunes, J.R. 2014. 'Success and failure of grassroots innovations for addressing climate change: The case of the TTM', *Global Environmental Change* 24, pp 232–250.

Geels, F. 2002. 'Technical transitions as evolutionary reconfiguration processes: A multi-level perspective and a case study', *Research Policy* 31, pp 1257–1274.

Gerland, P. *et al.* 2014. 'World population stabilization unlikely this century', *Science* 18 September 2014.

Gleeson, B. 2015. *The urban condition*, Routledge, New York.

Henfrey, T. and Kenrick, J. 2015. 'Climate, commons, and hope: The TTM in global perspective', http://climatesecurityagenda.org/wp-content/uploads/2015/11/018138c_TNI_Climate-Commons-Hope.pdf (accessed 6 June 2015).

Holmgren, D. 2002. *Permaculture: Principles and pathways beyond sustainability*, Holmgren Design Services, Hepburn.

Holmgren, D. 2012. 'Retrofitting the suburbs for an energy descent future', *Simplicity Institute Report* 12i, 1–9.

Hopkins, R. 2009. *The transition handbook: Creating local sustainable communities beyond oil dependency* (Australian and New Zealand Edition), Finch Publishing, Lane Cove, Australia.

Hopkins, R. 2011. *The transition companion: Making your community more resilient in uncertain time*, Chelsea Green Publishing, White River Junction, Vt.

Hopkins, R. 2013. *The power of just doing stuff: How local action can change the world*, UIT/Green Books, Cambridge.

Hopkins, R. and Miller, A. 2012. 'Climate after growth: Why environmentalists must embrace post-growth economics and community resilience', *Post-Carbon Institute Report*, pp 1–28.

SAMUEL ALEXANDER

Jenkins, J. 2005 (3rd edn). *The humanure handbook: A guide to composting human manure*, Chelsea Green Publishing, White River Junction, VT.

Kemp, R., Schot, J., and Hoogma, R. 1998. 'Regime shifts to sustainability through processes of niche formation: The approach of strategic niche management, *Technology Analysis & Strategic Management* 10(2), pp 175–198.

Longhurst, N. 2015. 'Towards an "alternative" geography of innovation: Alternative milieu, socio-cognitive protection and sustainability experimentation', *Environmental Innovation and Societal Transitions* 17, pp 183–198.

Loorbach, D. 2010. 'Transition management for sustainable development: A prescriptive, complexity-based governance framework', *Governance* 23(1), pp 161–183.

Louv, R. 2011. *The nature principle: Human restoration and the end of nature-deficit disorder*, Algonquin Books, New York.

Mason, K. and Whitehead, M. (2012) 'Transition urbanism and the contested politics of ethical place making', *Antipode* 44(2), pp 493–516.

Meadows, D., Randers, J., and Meadows, D., 2004. *Limits to growth: The 30-year update*, Chelsea Green Publishing, White River Junction, Vt.

Mohr, S. *et al.* 2015. 'Projection of world fossil fuels by country', *Fuels* 141, pp 120–135.

North, P. 2010. 'Eco-localisation as a progressive response to peak oil and climate change – a sympathetic critique, *Geoforum* 41, pp 585–594.

North, P. and Scott Cato, M. 2012. 'A suitable climate for political action? A sympathetic review of the politics of transition', in Pelling, M., Manuel-Navarrete, D., and Redclift, M. (eds). *Climate change and the crisis of capitalism: A chance to reclaim self, society and nature*, Routledge, London, pp 99–113.

Pelling M., Navarrete, D.M. 2011. 'From resilience to transformation: The adaptive cycle in two Mexican urban centers', *Ecology and Society* 16(2), http://www.ecologyandsociety.org/vol16/iss2/art11/ (accessed 15 January 2013).

Pinkerton, T. and Hopkins, R. 2009. *Local food: How to make it happen in your community*, Green Books, Totnes, Devon.

Roorda, C. *et al.* 2014. *Transition management in the urban context: Guidance manual*, DRIFT, Erasmus University, Rotterdam.

Rotmans, J., Kemp, R., and Asselt, M. 2001. 'More evolution than revolution: transition management in public policy', *Foresight* 3(1), pp 15–31.

Sanne, C. 2002. 'Willing consumers – or locked-in? Policies for sustainable consumption', *Ecological Economics* 42, pp 273–287.

74

Seyfang, G. and Haxeltine, A. 2012. 'Growing grassroots innovations: Exploring the role of community-based initiatives in governing sustainable energy transitions', *Environment and Planning C: Government and Policy* 30, pp 381–400.

Seyfang, G. and Smith, A. 2007. 'Grassroots innovations for sustainable development: Towards a new research and policy agenda', *Environmental Politics* 16(4), pp 584–603.

Shove, E. and Walker, G. 2007. 'CAUTION! Transitions ahead: Politics, practice and sustainable transition management, *Environment and Planning A* 39, pp 763–770.

Steffan, W., Richardson K., Rockstrom, J. *et al*. 2015. 'Planetary boundaries: Guiding human development on a change planet, *Science* 347(6623) (13 February 2015).

Sharp, N. 2014. 'The zillion year town', https://archive.org/details/TZYT1 (accessed 2 June 2016).

Smith, A. 2007. 'Translating sustainabilities between green niches and socio-technical regimes', *Technology Analysis & Strategic Management* 19(4), pp 427–450.

Taylor, P.J. 2012. 'Transition towns and world cities: Towards green networks of cities', *Local Environment* 17 (4), pp 495–508.

Trainer, T. 2010. *Transition to a just and sustainable world*, Envirobook, Sydney.

Trainer, T. 2014. 'Transition townspeople, we need to think about transition (Just doing stuff is far from enough!), http://thesimplerway.info/TRANSITIONERS.htm (accessed 3 June 2016).

Trainer, T. 2016. 'Remaking settlements: The potential cost reductions enabled by The Simpler Way'. *Simplicity Institute Report* 15e, pp 1–39.

Transition Network, 2016. 'Official initiatives by number', https://www.transitionnetwork.org/initiatives/by-number (accessed 6 June 2016).

Turner, G. 2014. 'Is global collapse imminent?' *MSSI Research Paper* No.4, Melbourne Sustainable Society Institute, pp 1–21.

Weidmann, T. *et al*. 2015. 'The material footprint of nations', *Proceedings of the National Academy of Sciences of the USA* 112(20), pp 6271–6276.

Wilson, G.A. 2012. 'Community resilience, globalization and transitional pathways of decision-making', *Geoforum* 43, pp 1218–1231.

Wolfram, A. 2017. *Grassroots niches in urban contexts: Exploring governance innovations for sustainable development in Seoul*, Procedia Engineering (in press).

4

THE DEGROWTH IMPERATIVE: RESPONDING TO THE CLIMATE EMERGENCY

1. Introduction*

This chapter provides a critical overview of rapidly evolving debates about the necessity and desirability of including planned and equitable 'degrowth' as an important component in global decarbonisation strategies. In doing so the chapter highlights and explores the tension between two apparently paradoxical propositions about the relationship between climate change solutions and economic growth.

The first proposition, as Lord Stern has reiterated in launching the *New Climate Economy Report* (see Global Commission on the Economy and Climate, 2014), is this: 'Reducing emissions is not only compatible with economic growth and development, if done well it can actually generate better growth than the old high-carbon model' (see Harvey, 2014).

The second proposition, informed by the inconvenient truth of carbon budget mathematics, is that decarbonisation at the speed and scale required to keep global warming below 2 degrees will also require a systematic, planned and equitable reduction in the consumption of energy and resources. Tyndall Centre climate change researchers Kevin Anderson and Alice

---

* This chapter was co-authored by Samuel Alexander and John Wiseman.

Bows summarise this argument in the following way: 'For a reasonable probability of avoiding the 2°C characterisation of dangerous climate change the wealthier nations need, temporarily, to adopt a de-growth strategy' (see Anderson, 2013).

This chapter therefore begins with an assessment of whether continued economic growth, in terms of GDP, is consistent with the necessary speed and scale of decarbonisation which is called for by carbon budget analyses. Those who argue that it is believe growth and a safe climate are compatible, provided there is a swift implementation of renewable energy, energy efficiency and low carbon land-use strategies, complemented by other policies, such as putting a price on carbon. The contrasting and more radical position, as Anderson and Bows argue, is that keeping to a fair share of the carbon budget now requires wealthy nations to implement those low carbon policies *but also* to undertake deliberate degrowth strategies of planned economic contraction (see Latouche, 2009; Kallis, 2011; Alexander, 2012a).

Not surprisingly, this latter conclusion – that a period of planned degrowth in consumption and production may be required to stay within carbon budget targets – has triggered strong debate (see, e.g., Victor, 2012; Hopkins and Miller, 2012; Grantham Institute, 2013; Global Commission on the Economy and Climate, 2014). The second section of our chapter therefore addresses five 'frequently asked questions' about the importance – and the challenges – of inserting alternative economic paradigms, such as degrowth, into mainstream conversations about climate change solutions.

2. Carbon Budget Targets: Implications for Economic Growth Goals and Paradigms

Recent analysis of the global resource depletion trends, first quantified forty years ago in *Limits to Growth* (Meadows *et al.*, 2004), combined with more recent work on the 'planetary boundaries' within which humanity can thrive (Rockstrom *et al.*, 2009), continues to indicate that business-as-usual consumption trends are driving significant risks of global economic collapse in the second half of this century, or earlier (Turner, 2012; Ehrlich and Ehrlich, 2013). More specifically, as the probability of catastrophic climate change continues to grow (Potsdam, 2012; Christoff, 2013), analysis of global carbon budget trends and targets provides grounds for thinking that carefully planned, equitable reductions in the global consumption of energy and resources may be required to meet the climate challenge. The controversial question is whether dealing with these crises adequately, and reducing energy demands sufficiently, is consistent with the growth paradigm that currently structures and informs macroeconomic thinking around the world (Purdey, 2010; Rezai, Taylor, and Mechler, 2013).

The concept of a 'carbon budget' (Le Quere *et al.*, 2014; Committee on Climate Change, 2013; Carbon Tracker, 2011; Messner *et al.*, 2010) refers to the total amount of carbon emissions that can be released into the atmosphere in order to retain a reasonable chance of avoiding 'dangerous' climate change (Mann, 2009; Anderson and Bows, 2011; Anderson, 2012). While there are, as noted below, a range of views about the global warming 'guard rail' consistent with avoiding dangerous climate change, current IPCC (2013, 2014) carbon budget calculations are based on the goal of keeping global temperature levels below a 2°C temperature rise above pre-industrial levels (see also, Meinhausen *et al.*, 2009; Macintosh, 2010).

The 2013 IPCC 5th Assessment Report concluded that, to achieve a greater than 66% chance of limiting warming to 2°C, a total of approximately 1000 gigatons of carbon dioxide can be emitted in the period following the beginning of the industrial revolution (IPCC, 2013: 27-8). As of 2011, approximately 515 gigatons had already been emitted. According to this analysis, continuation of business-as-usual emission rates would see the global carbon budget run out by around 2045. Increasing the probability of success to 80% or higher would mean the carbon budget would be consumed even sooner (see e.g., Carbon Tracker, 2011; Carbon Tracker and Grantham Institute, 2013). Delaying the date at which global emissions begin to be reduced would lead logically to the requirement for more rapid reductions in later years. Conversely, an earlier date at which more rapid emissions reductions begin would allow a more gradual path to overall emission reductions.

A growing array of decarbonisation roadmaps, such as the *UN Deep Decarbonisation Pathways Project* (SDSN and IDDRI, 2014) and the *New Climate Economy Report* (Global Commission on the Economy and Climate, 2014), demonstrate widespread agreement about the overall suite of technological and market initiatives needed to drive swift emissions reductions (for a review, see Wiseman, Edwards, and Luckins, 2013). The policy levers available to achieve these goals are now widely understood.

i)   Raising resource efficiency through direct government regulatory and legislative intervention; the replacement of subsidies to fossil fuel industries with incentives strengthening demand for renewable energy, energy efficiency, low emissions agriculture and carbon sequestration; and a robust price on carbon;
ii) Stimulating and driving a diverse mix of societal and technological innovations; and
iii) Mobilising the infrastructure investment needed to drive the transition to a just, equitable low carbon economy.

Swift implementation of many of the strategic priorities outlined in plans like *Pathways to Deep Decarbonisation* and the *New Climate Economy Report* will clearly form an essential basis for any comprehensive, equitable global decarbonisation strategy.

However, the increasingly large elephant in the room is that, as the *New Climate Economy Report* itself notes, there is still a large gap between the decarbonisation outcomes likely to result from these strategies and the actions needed to have a real chance of keeping global warming below 2 degrees. Here, for example, is what the *New Climate Economy Report* (Commission on the Economy and Climate, 2014: 10) says about the alignment between actions and targets:

> *Implementation of the policies and investments pro-*
> *posed in this report could deliver at least half of the*
> *reductions in emissions needed by 2030* to lower the
> risk of dangerous climate change. With strong and broad
> implementation, rapid learning and sharing of best prac-
> tice this number could potentially rise to 90%. *Further*
> *action would also be required.* Some of this, such as the
> development of carbon capture and storage technologies,
> will have net costs to be borne solely for the purpose of
> reducing climate risk. *Beyond 2040 net global emission*
> *will need to fall further* towards near zero or below in the
> second half of the century [italics added; bold emphasis
> removed].

A number of questions immediately arise: How can the widening
gap between proposed actions and required emissions reductions be closed? To what extent is it wise or prudent to build
long-term climate solutions that are so reliant on prohibitively
expensive and fundamentally unproven technologies such as
carbon capture and storage? And how can the formidable barriers
standing in the way of rapid, 'strong and broad implementation'
be overcome (see Rickards, Wiseman, Kashima, 2014)?

The case for including planned and equitable degrowth in
a comprehensive suite of decarbonisation strategies has been
most compellingly presented through the work of Kevin Anderson and Alice Bows in their January 2011 paper in the journal
Philosophical Transactions of the Royal Society, 'Beyond
Dangerous Climate Change: Emissions Scenarios for a New
World'. Anderson and Bows take as their starting point the
2009 Copenhagen Accord commitment to 'hold the increase in
global temperature below 2 degrees Celsius and take action to
meet this objective consistent with science and on the basis of
equity'. They then challenge us to carefully consider the implications of the following scenarios and assumptions on climate
change and economic growth expectations (see also, Anderson,
2013; Anderson and Bows, 2012; Anderson and Bows, 2008a;
Anderson and Bows, 2008b).

i) If our aim is to achieve decarbonisation targets consistent with a 50% probability of keeping global warming below 2 degrees;

ii) and we work on the (highly optimistic) assumption that the 'least developed economies' peak emissions by 2025 and then reduce their emissions by 7% per year;

iii) it then follows that developed economies will need to reduce emissions by 8-10% p.a. until zero emissions are approached or attained.

iv) However, mainstream economic analyses (e.g., Stern, 2006) consistently argue that emissions reductions of more than 3% or 4% p.a. are incompatible with economic growth.

v) It is therefore likely that developed economies will need to implement temporary policies of degrowth in consumption and production if there is to be a 50% probability of keeping global warming below 2 degrees.

While there are many variations in the precise way this scenario might unfold (depending, for example, on assumptions about the timing of peak emissions, probabilities of success, and the equity principles used to allocate national responsibilities), Anderson and Bows' core argument about the need to include degrowth in the debate about decarbonisation options demands serious consideration. 'We cannot get off the emissions curve fast enough through technology alone,' they argue. 'We have to change what it is we consume. Not just what we consume but the rates and levels of our consumption' (see Anderson and Wiseman, 2012: 4). This understanding of degrowth is consistent with the definition employed by Schneider *et al.* (2010: 512), who describe degrowth as 'an equitable down-scaling of production and consumption that increases human well-being and enhances ecological conditions.'

Two points of clarification are immediately called for here. First, we need to carefully distinguish the concept of *planned* reductions in consumption and production (i.e. 'degrowth') from *unplanned* economic contraction (i.e., 'recession'). This distinction highlights the difference between a future in which rapid reductions in energy and resource demands are achieved through a deliberative, equitable process as opposed to an alternative future in which consumption crashes as a result of *unplanned* economic collapse. Peter Victor (2008) describes the move beyond growth as being possible by either 'design or disaster', a description that can be used to highlight the important distinction between degrowth, on the one hand, and recession/ depression/ collapse, on the other.

Secondly, the transition to a zero carbon, degrowth economy is likely to require expansion in some sectors (such as renewable energy) as well as accelerated 'degrowth' in other sectors (such as aviation, fashion, luxury goods, etc.). As argued below, degrowth in the consumption of energy and resources might also be consistent with 'growth' in health and wellbeing or in the time available to care for children and the elderly (see generally, Odum and Odum, 2001; Jackson, 2009; Bilancini and D'Alessandro, 2012; Alexander, 2012b; Diffenbaugh, 2013; Kubiszewski *et al.*, 2013). It is also assumed that there may need to be 'growth' of some form in the Global South in order to attain a dignified quality of life for all, so calls for degrowth should be understood to be directed primarily at the wealthy and most developed nations. At the same time, it is critical to emphasise that any adequate response to climate change will require the Global South to avoid the high-carbon development path which would also burst the carbon budget by locking poorer nations into decades of high-carbon living.

3. Decarbonisation and Degrowth: Frequently Asked Questions and Key Debates

The argument that downscaling of production and consumption should be a core component in the implementation of comprehensive decarbonisation strategies often triggers strong reactions – such as Nobel Laureate Paul Krugman's (2014) recent *New York Times* critique: 'The idea that economic growth and climate action are incompatible may sound hardheaded and realistic, but it's actually a fuzzy-minded misconception.' The following reflections are therefore designed to respond to five of the most common criticisms of the argument that climate science requires careful consideration of the case for degrowth.

3.1 Are the global warming and carbon budget targets underpinning the case for planned degrowth overstated or understated?

One of the most compelling features of the case for degrowth is the cautious and conservative assumptions about decarbonisation targets underpinning scenarios and propositions such as those outlined by Anderson and Bows (2011).

The data on which their argument is constructed was originally published in 2011. Since then the emissions reduction challenge has in fact become even tougher with the 2014 *Global Carbon Budget* update (Le Quere *et al.*, 2014) confirming that global carbon dioxide emissions grew by 2.3 per cent to a record annual high of 36.1 billion tonnes CO_2 in 2013. Even a 'peak' in emissions will be of little solace unless deep and swift reductions in emissions follow.

As the most recent UNEP *Emissions Gap Report* also notes the 2030 'emissions gap', defined as the difference between global emission levels consistent with the 2°C target versus the emissions levels expected if current national cases are extrapolated to 2030, is 14–17 Gt CO2e (i.e., about a third of current global emissions).

While few climate scientists advocate a global warming target above 2 degrees, many express grave concern about consequences for the health and wellbeing of human beings and other species of global warming above 2 degrees (Jordan *et al.*, 2013; Christoff, 2013). Noting also the escalating risks of triggering key climatic tipping points, many indeed argue for a target of 1.5 degrees or below with the aim, over time, of reducing global temperatures to pre-industrial levels (for a review, see Spratt, 2014a; Spratt, 2014b). If this analysis is correct then the global carbon budget is already spent, or close to spent. This conclusion would further reinforce the case for including degrowth goals in a comprehensive suite of decarbonisation initiatives.

The goal of a 50% probability of keeping global warming below 2 degrees is also extremely conservative given that the Copenhagen Accord commitment of a *low* to *very low* chance of exceeding 2°C would normally imply a probability of staying under 2 degrees warming of 90% or above. The assumption that emissions from less developed economies might peak by 2025 and then decrease at an unprecedented rate of 7% pa is also extremely optimistic. Extrapolation of current emissions trends indicates that this outcome remains extremely challenging and suggests that Anderson and Bows' case for considering some level of 'degrowth' in the wealthiest, highest emitting economies is in fact based on very moderate premises indeed.

3.2 Will existing technological solutions be sufficient to stay within the global carbon budget?

As Ronald Reagan's seductively reassuring response to *Limits to Growth* reminds us, blind faith in the capability of technical and engineering solutions to deliver climate change 'magic bullets' continues to be a formidable barrier to honest appraisal of the actions needed to fully address carbon budget challenges. 'There are no great limits to growth,' Reagan cheerfully explained, 'because there are no limits of human intelligence, imagination, and wonder' (Cider Mill Press, 2012: 2). Exxon CEO Rex Tillerson's bald assertion that climate change is 'an engineering problem and it has engineering solutions' (Daily, 2012: np) is a more recent example of the pervasive influence of such self-serving techno-optimism.

The pace of technological innovation in renewable energy, energy efficiency and low carbon land use is impressive and encouraging. Breakthroughs in battery storage, smart grids, and distributed systems now demonstrate real potential to address renewable energy baseload and intermittency issues (Diesendorf, 2014), although questions remain (see Trainer, 2013a; Trainer 2013b). The extraordinary acceleration in Chinese renewable energy production is also driving down solar and wind energy costs significantly, and advances in digital printing continue to bring forward the prospect of transformational change in the energy intensity of manufacturing and transport.

While formidable renewable energy challenges remain (such as the replacement of liquid fuels for shipping and aviation) these promising developments are useful reminders of the extent to which technological innovation will clearly play a *necessary* and central role in rapid emission reductions. However there also are a number of important reasons why technological innovation alone is unlikely to provide a *sufficient* basis for addressing carbon budget challenges at the required speed and scale.

The first heroic assumption underpinning techno-optimist solutions is the ongoing reliance in many of the most influential large-scale decarbonisation strategies on Carbon Capture and Storage (CCS). While CCS may play a valuable, albeit modest, long-term role, the current state of knowledge suggests that we are still a very long way from affordable and scalable CCS deployment. Even the Global CCS Institute (2013: 5) has recently reported that, 'while CCS projects are progressing, the pace is well below the level required for CCS to make substantial contribution to climate change mitigation'. The growing 'emissions gap' is also providing increasing impetus for speculation about the 'necessity' of geo-engineering 'solutions' with all their attendant concerns about ethical implications and unintended consequences (see Hamilton, 2013).

The second debatable assumption is that technological innovation will necessarily and rapidly translate into global reductions in energy consumption. Important questions remain about the speed with which 100 percent renewable energy can realistically be achieved (see, e.g., Smil, 2010; Smil, 2014); the extent of fossil fuel energy consumption required to drive the initial massive expansion in renewable energy infrastructure; and the full life cycle energy return on investment (EROI) outcomes of solar and wind energy – particularly if these calculations factor in the full costs of energy storage (see, e.g., Palmer, 2012; Prieto and Hall, 2013). Noting that emissions reductions of 4 percent pa in an economy growing at 2 percent pa are likely to require carbon intensity improvements of around 6 percent pa., Anderson (2013) notes that he has yet to find any credible main-stream economist prepared to argue that prolonged emissions reductions of 3% or 4% or more are compatible with economic growth.

Indeed, as Lord Stern (2006: 231) himself has noted:

> There is likely to be a maximum practical rate at which global emissions can be reduced. At the national level, there are examples of sustained emissions cuts of up to 1% per year associated with structural change in energy systems ... whilst maintaining strong economic growth. However, cuts in emissions greater than this have historically been associated only with economic recession or upheaval, for example, the emissions reduction of 5.2% per year for a decade associated with the economic transition and strong reduction in output in the former Soviet Union. These magnitudes of cuts suggest it is likely to be very challenging to reduce emissions by more than a few percent per year while maintaining strong economic growth.

The third reason for caution in assuming overly optimistic relationships between technological innovation, carbon intensity and emissions reductions is the impact of the 'rebound effect' (see Jevons, 1865; Herring and Sorrell, 2009; Holm and Englund, 2009; Jackson, 2009). This phenomenon refers to the tendency for innovation and efficiency gains to be rapidly overwhelmed as cheaper unit costs combined with the formidable reach and power of the global advertising industry enables and encourages individuals to consume more of the same or alternative services and products. The harsh reality remains that global emissions continue to grow (IPCC, 2013) – along with the global trends in the consumption of energy and resources – with apparent improvements in developed economy energy efficiency often masking the reality of energy intensive production being offshored to developing economies.

The likelihood of full and fast deployment of new technologies is the fourth problematic assumption that needs to be addressed given the formidable political and social obstacles standing in the way of rapid implementation. As noted in the recent *Post Carbon Pathways* review of learning from the implementation of large scale decarbonisation strategies (see Wiseman, Edwards, Luckins, 2013), experienced climate scientists and policy makers consistently come to the conclusion that the key obstacles standing in the way of rapid decarbonisation are political and social rather than technological. Key roadblocks include the following:

- Climate scepticism and denial of the necessity and urgency of action
- The power and influence of vested interests in the fossil fuel, finance, and media industries
- Extreme individualist and neo-liberal values and ideologies
- Inequitable distribution of emission reduction costs and responsibilities
- Technological, social, and economic path dependencies
- Financial and governance constraints

3.3 How can the global social equity and economic wellbeing implications of a deliberate reduction in energy and resource consumption be addressed?

Implementing decarbonisation solutions which are fundamentally equitable in terms of current and historical emission responsibilities as well as current income and wealth distribution is essential from both an ethical and strategic point of view. This is why Anderson and Bows (2011) and other degrowth advocates (see generally, D'Alisa, Demaria, and Kallis, 2014; Lawn and Clarke, 2010) place such emphasis on the need for the wealthiest citizens in the wealthiest economies to take on the heavy lifting in relation to reducing consumption.

The first response to criticisms of degrowth strategies based on professed concern for impacts on the poorest communities is of the same order as the response to the disingenuous arguments sometimes heard from mining executives about the impact of cutting coal exports on the poor of India or Africa. The impacts of catastrophic climate change (see Potsdam, 2012) on the most vulnerable populations will surely be vastly greater than the impacts of even the most rapid emissions reductions policies. It will also be far easier to ensure that the impacts of reduction in economic growth are managed in an equitable way if the reductions are brought about through a process of planned contraction rather than a sudden and unplanned slide into recession or depression.

George Monbiot's (2014) reflections on the distributional costs and benefits of the current growth paradigm are also highly relevant here.

> One of the remarkable characteristics of recent growth in the rich world is how few people benefit. Almost all the gains go to a tiny number of people: one study suggests that the richest 1% in the United States capture 93% of the increase incomes that growth delivers. Even with growth rates of 2 or 3% or more, working conditions for most people continue to deteriorate, as we find ourselves on short contracts, without full employment rights, without the security or the choice or the pensions their parents enjoyed.

While it is ethically and strategically crucial that developed economies take primary responsibility for the initial peak and decline in emissions (Gardiner, 2011), it is also essential that less developed economies begin the transition to a zero-carbon economy pathway as soon as possible (Anderson and Bows, 2008b). It will therefore be vital that less developed nations are given increased support to create low-carbon economies *now*, rather than follow fossil fuel-based development pathways that 'lock' societies into decades of high-carbon living. Any equitable pathway to global decarbonisation therefore needs to deliver sustained financial commitments from the most developed to the least developed economies to support technology transfer, structural adjustment and climate resilience strategies. This is even truer of decarbonisation strategies which include a significant emphasis on planned reduction in global consumption.

An additional important priority for degrowth advocates will be the design of transition strategies which address the very real concerns of vulnerable workers and communities about employment implications. Reductions in overall paid working hours, the exploration of a variety of forms of basic or guaranteed income and structural adjustment policies targeted to meet the challenges facing workers in industries likely to be downscaled (such as coal mining) will all be part of this crucial conversation.

3.4 Will raising the case for 'degrowth' undermine political support for decisive climate action?

Some supporters of decisive climate action might be unsettled by public debate about the inclusion of planned reductions in economic output in a comprehensive decarbonisation strategy, but this is not an argument for staying silent about the full risks and implications of climate science. It is, however, an important reminder of the need to ensure that arguments about alternative economic growth paradigms are framed in ways which maximise resonance and impact.

While the goal of 'planned and equitable degrowth' works well for some audiences, the language of a 'wellbeing' or 'sufficiency' economy may be useful in demonstrating the desirability of economic paradigms focused on growing health and wellbeing for the many rather than endless acceleration in energy and resource consumption for the few. As the authors of the *Limits to Growth* (2005: 11-12) report remind us:

> A sustainable society [does not] need to be stagnant, boring, uniform, or rigid....It could be a world that has the time, the resources, and the will to correct its mistakes, to innovate, to preserve the fertility of its planetary ecosystems. It could focus on mindfully increasing quality of life rather than on mindlessly expanding material consumption and the physical capital stock.

While care is required to avoid romanticising poverty and inequality, evidence also continues to grow that, beyond a relatively modest level of income, growth in average subjective wellbeing levels off (see Alexander, 2012b). Once core material needs are met, non-material priorities such as reduced stress; more time with friends and family, and more meaningful and creative work become increasingly important (see generally, Helliwell, Layard, Sachs, 2013). Accordingly, the goal of a 'wellbeing economy' (see, e.g., Diener and Seligman, 2004) has the potential to be framed as a desirable alternative to the psychological stresses and ecological risks of a growth obsessed economy. Alternative progress and wellbeing indicator frameworks – such as the Genuine Progress Indicator, the OECD Better Life Index or the Bhutanese Gross National Happiness framework – can play a valuable role in providing tangible reality to these alternative economic paradigms (see generally, Costanza *et al.*, 2014; Kubiszewski *et al.*, 2013; Royal Government of Bhutan, 2012; Stiglitz, Sen, and Fitoussi, 2010; Lawn 2006).

In the end, however, this debate reflects two competing views about climate change solutions and political strategy. One view is that the first priority must be to secure broad popular support for at least some level of significant emissions reduction, in the hope that, once the process is underway, the momentum will rapidly accelerate. The alternative view is that it is preferable to build political support for comprehensive climate change solutions on the basis of an honest appraisal of scientific evidence and the full magnitude of the challenge rather on wishful thinking or an implausibly optimistic reliance on technological silver bullets. It is critical that a coherent climate solution is expressed in a way that engages as many people as possible; at the same time, it is no good engaging a wide audience if that means presenting a false or misleading picture of what a genuine climate solution or response looks like. If one should call a spade a spade, perhaps one should call for degrowth if that indeed is the clearest description of what is required. This is a debate that may have no single right answer, but it is clear that the issues under consideration are of the highest importance and deserve close attention.

3.5 What political strategies could plausibly build broad support for rapid and comprehensive reductions in consumption and production?

Any plausible pathway towards equitable degrowth will need to be built on the same mix of transformational change strategies required to remove the political and structural roadblocks standing in the way of overall solutions to the climate crisis: education and evidence; ethical and moral persuasion; disruptive social and technological innovation; citizen mobilisation; visionary and courageous leadership; and decisive action at moments of ecological, economic, and social crisis.

To date the primary social change focus of many degrowth advocates has been on building the ethical and moral case for low-consumption lifestyles and through the politics of prefigurative action and example: of driving and flying less and cycling and walking more; of Transition towns and permaculture; of growing and sharing local food; of retrofitting our houses for energy efficiency; of wearing warmer clothing rather than turning on heaters; of recycling, making and mending things rather than buying new; and of generally trying to build a more localised, egalitarian, and low-carbon society from the grassroots up.

Actions at the personal, household, and community levels will be an important and surely necessary foundation for broader cultural change but are likely to remain small scale and marginal without systematic work to address key social and physical constraints limiting the adoption of sustainable consumption lifestyles (e.g., Sanne, 2002). It is, for example, hard to drive less in the absence of safe bike lanes and good public transport; it is hard to find a work-life balance if access to basic housing burdens us with excessive debt; and it is hard to re-imagine a way of life built on reduced consumption if we are constantly bombarded with advertisements insisting that 'nice stuff' is the key to happiness.

Therefore, a fully scalable, mainstreamed strategy for

building a low consumption economy may also require a far more proactive role for government leadership and policy intervention, although it may be that such 'top down' leadership arrives only *after* there has been a deep cultural shift (Alexander, 2013). In reflecting on the possibilities of courageous high-level leadership it is interesting to reflect on the preparedness of a former US president, Jimmy Carter, in 1979, to openly question the dominant values of consumerist culture.

> Too many of us now tend to worship self-indulgence and consumption. Human identity is no longer defined by what one does, but by what one owns. But we've discovered that owning things and consuming things does not satisfy our longing for meaning. We've learned that piling up material goods cannot fill the emptiness of lives which have no confidence or purpose (Carter, 1979: np).

The ferocious political response to Carter's so-called 'malaise speech' certainly alerts us to the storm of hostility and ridicule which is likely to erupt around anyone attempting to lead public debate about alternative economic and consumption paradigms. The strategic advice often attributed to Mahatma Gandhi may be relevant to remember here: 'First they ignore you, then they laugh at you, then they fight you, then you win.'

As influential contributors to the emerging literature on post-growth economic policy paradigms such as Tim Jackson (2009) and Peter Victor (2008) note, the first step in achieving a rapid and equitable transition to a post-growth, post-carbon economy will be the adoption of an integrated framework of social, ecological, and economic wellbeing goals, targets, and indicators reflecting an explicit commitment to this goal. Implementation strategies and policies consistent with this goal are likely to include the following:

i) Taxation, income security and pension policies driving an equitable, economy-wide shift from consumption to savings.

ii) Deployment of the institutions and incentives needed to build a fully circular, zero waste economy.

iii) Financial institutions and regulatory frameworks capable of mobilising savings into post-carbon economy infrastructure and industry investments.

iv) Urban design, housing, freight, and public transport systems enabling more localised economic relationships and transactions.

v) Labour market and income security policies facilitating a rapid shift to shorter working hours.

vi) Structural adjustment policies which address employment and income issues for vulnerable workers and communities.

As writers like Jackson and Victor also rightly note, there is still considerable work to be done to construct a coherent body of economic policies capable of delivering an equitable agenda of post-growth, ecological economics (but see, Kallis, Kerschner, Martinez-Alier, 2012). This task, along with strengthening understanding of the most effective ways of developing a low consumption culture, are two of the highest research and policy priorities which sustainability campaigners concerned with building informed support for degrowth strategies might usefully begin to focus on.

4. Conclusion

Our overall argument can be summarised in the following way. The core implication from all of the most recent analyses of carbon emissions trends is clear. Swift implementation of even the most ambitious renewable energy, energy efficiency, and low-carbon land use measures will still fall well short of the emissions reductions needed to stay within the global carbon budget (UNEP, 2014). This gap can be bridged in three main ways:

1. Gambling on leap-of-faith mitigation technologies such as biofuels, carbon capture and storage, nuclear fusion, and geo-engineering.
2. Gambling on the even more unlikely leap of faith that adaptation to global temperatures of 4 degrees and above is possible.
3. Reducing the consumption of energy and resources by the wealthiest people in the wealthiest countries. Importantly, this is the only option which also addresses other urgent global ecological challenges such as ocean acidification, the collapse of biodiversity – and the equitable distribution of increasingly scarce resources.

Many complex and contested questions remain.

• How should we balance overall reductions in consumption with the expansions in production in the industry sectors required to build a zero carbon economy?
• How precisely should we define, describe, and deliver planned and equitable degrowth?
• What set of arguments and circumstances could plausibly achieve popular support for degrowth policies in the wealthiest economies?

The important point, however – and the key point of this chapter – is to argue the case for including planned and equitable reductions in the consumption of energy and resources in debates about the suite of actions needed to meet global climate change and planetary boundary challenges. In preparing this chapter we have been very conscious that imagining a degrowth society is almost as hard as imagining a zero carbon global economy. We have therefore kept in mind Nelson Mandela's reflections on a very different by equally formidable challenge: 'It always seems impossible until it is done.'

References

Alexander, S. 2012a. 'Planned economic contraction: The emerging case for degrowth', *Environmental Politics* 21(3), pp 349–368.

Alexander, S. 2012b. 'The optimal material threshold: Toward an economics of sufficiency', *Real-World Economics Review* 61, pp 2–21.

Alexander, S. 2013b. 'Voluntary simplicity and the social reconstruction of law: Degrowth from the grassroots up', *Environmental Values* 22(2), pp 287–308.

Anderson, K. 2012. 'Climate change going beyond dangerous – Brutal numbers and tenuous hope', *Development Dialogue* 61, pp 16–40.

Anderson, K. 2013. 'Avoiding dangerous climate change demands de-growth strategies from wealthier nations', available at: http://kevinanderson.info/blog/avoiding-dangerous-climate-change-demands-de-growth-strategies-from-wealthier-nations/ (accessed 1 February 2014).

Anderson, K. and Bows, A. 2008a. 'Reframing the climate change challenge in light of post-2000 emissions trends', *Philosophical Transactions of the Royal Society* 366, pp 3863–3882.

Anderson, K. and Bows, A. 2008b. 'Contraction and convergence: An assessment of the COOptions model', *Climatic Change* 91, pp 275–290.

Anderson, K. and Bows, A. 2011. 'Beyond "dangerous" climate change: Emission scenarios for a new world', *Philosophical Transactions of the Royal Society* 369, pp 20–44.

Anderson, K. and Bows, A. 2012. 'A new paradigm for climate change', *Nature Climate Change* 2, pp 639–640.

Anderson, K. and Wiseman, J. 2012. 'We need the courage to seek and develop a new paradigm: An interview with Kevin Anderson' (31 July 2012), available at: http://www.postcarbonpathways.net.au/wp-content/uploads/2013/05/KA_Interview.pdf (accessed 15 November 2014).

Ayres, R. and Warr, B. 2009. *The economic growth engine: How energy and work drive material prosperity*, Edward Elgar, Cheltenham.

Bilancini, E. and D'Alessandro, S. 2012. 'Long-run welfare under externalities in consumption, leisure, and production: A case for happy degrowth vs. unhappy growth', *Ecological Economics* 84, pp 194–205.

Carbon Tracker. 2011. 'Unburnable carbon: Are the world's financial markets carrying a carbon bubble?', available at: http://www.carbontracker.org/wp-content/uploads/2014/09/Unburnable-Carbon-Full-rev2-1.pdf (accessed 20 February 2014).

Carbon Tracker and Grantham Institute. 2013. 'Unburnable carbon 2013: Wasted capital and stranded assets' available at: http://carbontracker.

live.kiln.it/Unburnable-Carbon-2-Web-Version.pdf (accessed 15 July 2014).

Carter, J. 1979. 'Crisis of confidence' (presidential speech delivered on 15 July 1979), available at: http://www.cartercenter.org/news/editorials_speeches/crisis_of_confidence.html (accessed 15 November 2014).

Marchi, J. (ed.) 2010. *The deepest and noblest aspirations: The wisdom of Ronald Regan*, Cider Mill Press, Kennebunkport.

Christoff, P. (ed.) 2013. *Four degrees of global warming*, Taylor and Francis, London.

Committee on Climate Change, 2013. 'The Fourth Carbon Budget Review – Part 1', available at: http://www.theccc.org.uk/publication/fourth-carbon-budget-review-part-1/ (accessed 15 July 2013).

Costanza, R., Kubiszewski, I., Giovannini, E., *et al.* 2014. 'Time to Leave GDP Behind', *Nature* 505, pp 283–285.

Daily, M. 2012. 'Exxon CEO calls climate change an engineering problem', *Reuters* (27 June 2012), available at: http://www.reuters.com/article/2012/06/27/us-exxon-climate-idUSBRE85Q1C820120627 (accessed 15 November 2014).

D'Alisa, G., Demaria, F., and Kallis, G. 2014. *Degrowth: A vocabulary for a new era*, Routledge, London.

Diener, E. and Seligman, M. 2004. 'Beyond money: Toward an economy of well-being', *Psychological Science in the Public Interest* 5, pp 1–31.

Diesendorf, M. 2014. *Sustainable energy solutions for climate change*, Routledge, New York.

Diffenbaugh, N. 2013. 'Human well-being, the global emissions debt, and climate change commitment', *Sustainability Science* 8, pp 135–141.

Ehrlich, P. and Ehrlich A. 2013. 'Can a collapse of civilization be avoided?' *Simplicity Institute Report* 13a: 1–19.

Gardiner, S. 2011. *A perfect moral storm: The ethical tragedy of climate change*, Oxford University Press, Oxford.

Global Commission on the Economy and Climate. 2014. *Better growth, better climate: The new climate economy report* (the synthesis report), available at: http://static.newclimateeconomy.report/wp-content uploads/2014/08/NCE-SYNTHESIS-REPORT-web-share.pdf (accessed 15 November 2014).

Grantham Institute for Climate Change. 2013. 'Halving global CO2 by 2050: Technologies and costs', available at: http://www3.imperial.ac.uk/climatechange/publications/collaborative/halving-global-co2-by-2050 (accessed 1 February 2014);

Hamilton, C. 2013. *Earthmasters: Playing God with the climate*, Allen and Unwin, Crows Nest, NSW.

Harvey, F. 2014. 'Climate change report: Prevent damage by overhauling global economy', *The Guardian* (16 September 2014).

Helliwell, J., Layard, R., and Sachs, J. (eds). 2013. *World Happiness Report 2013*, available at: http://unsdsn.org/wp-content/uploads/2014/02/WorldHappinessReport2013_online.pdf (accessed 15 November 2014)

Herring, H. and Sorrell, S. 2009. *Energy efficiency and sustainable consumption: The rebound effect*, Palgrave Macmillan, London.

Hopkins, R. and Miller, A. 2012. 'Climate after growth: Why environmentalists must embrace post-growth economics and community resilience', *Post-Carbon Institute Report,* pp 1–28.

Holm, S.-O. and G. Englund. 2009. 'Increased ecoefficiency and gross rebound effect: Evidence from USA and six European countries 1960–2002', *Ecological Economics* 68, pp 879–887.

Intergovernmental Panel on Climate Change (IPCC). 2013. 'Climate Change 2013: The physical science basis (Fifth Assessment Report), available at: http://www.ipcc.ch/report/ar5/wg1/ (accessed 1 August 2014).

Intergovernmental Panel on Climate Change (IPCC). 2014. 'Climate Change 2014: Impacts, adaptations, and vulnerability (Fifth Assessment Report), available at: http://www.ipcc.ch/report/ar5/wg2/ (accessed 1 August 2014)

Jackson, T. 2009. *Prosperity without growth: Economics for a finite planet*, Earthscan, London.

Jevons, W.S. 1865. *The coal question: An inquiry concerning the progress of the nation and the probable exhaustion of our coal-mines*, MacMillan, London.

Jordan, A., Rayner, T., and Schroeder, H. *et al.* 2013. 'Going beyond two degrees? The risks and opportunities of alternative options', *Climate Policy* 13(6), pp 751–769.

Kallis, G. 2011. 'In defence of degrowth', *Ecological Economics* 70, pp 873–80.

Kallis, G., Kerschner, C., Martinez-Alier, J. 2012. 'The economics of degrowth', *Ecological Economics* 84, pp 172–180.

Kasser, T. 2002. *The high price of materialism*, MIT Press, Cambridge, Mass.

Krugman, P. 2014. 'Errors and omissions: Could fighting global warming be cheap and free?', *New York Times* (18 September 2014), available at: http://www.nytimes.com/2014/09/19/opinion/paul-krugman-could-fighting-global-warming-be-cheap-and-free.html?_r=0 (accessed 15 November 2014).

Kubiszewski, I., Costanza, R., Franco, C., *et al.* 2013. 'Beyond GDP: Measuring and achieving global genuine progress', *Ecological Economics* 93, pp 57–68.

Latouche, S. 2009. *Farewell to Growth,* Polity Press, Cambridge, UK.

Lawn, P. 2006. *Sustainable Development Indicators in Ecological Economics,* Edward Elgar, Cheltenham.

Lawn, P. and Clarke, M. 2010. 'The end of economic growth? A contracting threshold hypothesis', *Ecological Economics* 69, pp 2213–2223.

Le Quere, C. *et al.* 2014. 'Global Carbon Budget 2014', *Earth Systems Science Data* 7, pp 521–610.

Macintosh, A. 2010. 'Keeping warming within the 2C limit after Copenhagen', *Energy Policy* 38, pp 2964–2975.

Mann, M.E., 2009. 'Defining dangerous anthropogenic interference', *Proceedings of the National Academy of Science USA* 106, pp 4065–4066.

McKibben, B. 2012. 'Global warming's terrifying new math', *Rolling Stone,* 19 July 2012, available at: http://www.rollingstone.com/politics/news/global-warmings-terrifying-new-math-20120719 (accessed 1 February 2014).

Meadows, D., Randers, J., and Meadows, D. 2005. *Limits to growth: The 30-year update,* Earthscan, London.

Meinshausen, M., Meinshausen, N., Hare, W., *et al.* 2009. 'Greenhouse-gas emission targets for limiting global warming to 2-degrees', *Nature* 458, pp 1158–1162.

Messner, D., Schellnhuber, J., Rahmstorf, S., and Klingenfeld, D. 2010. 'The budget approach: A framework for a global transformation toward a low-carbon economy', *Journal of Renewable and Sustainable Energy* 2, pp 1–14.

Monbiot, G. 2014. 'It's time to shout stop on this war on the living world', *Guardian* (2 October 2014) available at: http://www.theguardian.com/environment/georgemonbiot/2014/oct/01/george-monbiot-war-on-the-living-world-wildlife (accessed 15 November 2014).

Odum, H. and Odum, E. 2001. *A prosperous way down: Principles and policies,* University of Colorado Press, Colorado.

Palmer, G. 2013. 'Household solar voltaics: Supplier of marginal abatement, or primary source of low-emissions power?' *Sustainability* 5(4), pp 1406–1442.

Potsdam Institute, 2012. *Turn down the heat: Why a 4° warmer world must be avoided,* published by the World Bank, available at: http://documents.worldbank.org/curated/en/2012/11/17097815/turn-down-heat-4%C2%B0c-warmer-world-must-avoided (accessed 15 July 2014).

Prieto, P. and Hall, C. 2013. *Spain's photovoltaic revolution: The energy return on investment,* Springer, New York.

Purdey, S. 2010. *Economic growth, the environment, and international relations: The growth paradigm*, Routledge, New York.

Rezai, A., Taylor, L., Mechler, R. 2013. 'Ecological macroeconomics: An application to climate change', *Ecological Economics* 85, pp 69–76.

Rickards, L., Wiseman, J., Kashima, Y. 2014. 'Barriers to effective climate change mitigation: The case of senior government and business decision makers', *Wiley Interdisciplinary Reviews: Climate Change* 5(6), 753–773.

Rockstrom, J., *et al.* 2009. 'Planetary boundaries: Exploring the safe operating space for humanity', *Ecology and Society* 14(2), Article 32.

Royal Government of Bhutan. 2012. 'The report of the high-level meeting on wellbeing and happiness: A new economic paradigm', available at: http://www.2apr.gov.bt/images/BhutanReport_WEB_F.pdf (accessed 14 December, 2013).

Sanne, C. 2002. 'Willing consumers – or locked in? Policies for a sustainable consumption', *Ecological Economics*, 42, pp 273–287.

Schneider, F., Kallis, G., and Martinez-Alier, J. 2010. 'Crisis or opportunity? Economic degrowth for social equity and ecological sustainability', *Journal of Cleaner Production* 18(6), pp 511–518.

Smil, V. 2010. *Energy transitions: History, requirements, prospects*, Praeger, Westport.

Smil, V. 2014. 'The long, slow rise of solar and wind', *Scientific American* 310, pp 52–57.

Spratt, D. 2014a. 'The real budgetary emergency and the myth of "burnable carbon"', *Climate Code Red*, 22 May 2014, available at: http://www.climatecodered.org/2014/05/the-real-budgetary-emergency-burnable.html (accessed 28 July 2014).

Spratt, D. 2014b. 'Carbon budgets, climate sensitivity, and the myth of burnable carbon', *Climate Code Red*, 8 June, 2014, available at: http://www.climatecodered.org/2014/06/carbon-budgets-climate-sensitivity-and.html (accessed 28 July 2014).

Stern, N. 2006. *Stern review on the economics of climate change*, Her Majesty's Treasury, Cambridge University Press, Cambridge.

Stiglitz, J., Sen, A., and Fitoussi, J.P., 2010. *Mis-measuring our lives: Why GDP doesn't add up*, The New Press, New York.

Sustainable Development Solutions Network (SDSN) and Institute for Sustainable Development and International Relations (IDDRI). 2014. 'Pathways to deep decarbonisation: Interim 2014 report', published by the SDSN and IDDRI (July 2014).

Trainer, T. 2013a. 'Can Europe run on renewable energy? A negative case', *Energy Policy* 63, pp 845–850.

Trainer, T. 2013b. 'Can the world run on renewable energy', *Humanomics* 29(2), pp: 88–104.

Turner, G., 2012. 'On the cusp of global collapse? Updated comparison of the *Limits to Growth* with historical data', *Gaia*, 21(2), pp 116–124.

United Nations Environment Program (UNEP). 2014. 'The Emissions Gap Report 2014: Synthesis', available at: http://www.unep.org/publications/ebooks/emissionsgapreport2014/portals/50268/pdf/EGR2014_EXECUTIVE_SUMMARY.pdf (accessed 25 November 2014).

Victor, P. 2008. *Managing without growth: Slower by design, not disaster*, Edward Elgar, Cheltenham, UK.

Victor, P. 2012. 'Growth, degrowth, and climate change: A scenario analysis', *Ecological Economics* 84, pp 206–212.

Wiseman, J., Edwards, T., and Luckins, K. 2013. *Post carbon pathways: Toward a just and resilient post carbon future*, CDP Discussion Paper, April 2013, available at: http://www.postcarbonpathways.net.au/wp-content/uploads/2013/05/Post-Carbon-Pathways-Report-2013_Final-V.pdf (accessed 1 July 2014).

5

VOLUNTARY SIMPLICITY AND THE STEADY-STATE ECONOMY

1. Introduction*

The inner crisis of our civilisation must be resolved
if the outer crisis is to be effectively met.
– Lewis Mumford

The 'voluntary simplicity' movement can be understood broadly as a diverse social movement made up of people who are resisting high-consumption lifestyles and who are seeking, in various ways, to minimise consumption while maintaining or even increasing quality of life. These downshifters, as they are sometimes called, are motivated by a range of personal, social, and environmental goals. It is timely to inquire into what role this movement may need to play in any successful transition to a steady state economy.

In this chapter we examine the notion of voluntary simplicity and suggest that any successful transition beyond the growth economy will depend in part on voluntary simplicity practices and values fundamentally reshaping consumer cultures. By doing so, the movement can provide the cultural conditions necessary for a steady state economy to take root. Indeed, we

---

* This chapter was co-authored by Samuel Alexander and Mark. A. Burch.

will argue that voluntary simplicity provides some of the cultural, psychological, and even philosophical underpinnings of the steady state economy, such that these mutually supportive movements will need to depend on and shape each other in important ways.

2. What is Voluntary Simplicity?

Let us begin by more fully defining the core concept. 'Voluntary simplicity' is characterised by the practices of mindfulness and material sufficiency (Elgin 2010; Burch 2000). Mindfulness can be understood as critical self-reflection on one's actions, values, relationships, attitudes, and habits with the aim of deliberately shaping or reshaping one's life in accordance with a conscious vision or purpose. By bringing mindfulness to our daily lives, those who practice voluntary simplicity seek the maximum of wellbeing achievable through the minimum of material consumption. Wellbeing applies to all life forms on Earth, not just people.

Sufficiency implies conscious moderation of material consumption to some admittedly flexible limit discerned by weighing both physical needs and ethical principles. Voluntary simplicity is about seeking and providing enough, for everyone, forever. Given that we live in an age of gross ecological overshoot and growing population, a truly sustainable way of life turns out to be a radical project, going far beyond merely recycling, taking shorter showers, and turning off the lights (see Trainer 2010). To achieve one planet living, the practice of sufficiency must replace the pursuit of affluence in consumer cultures, with voluntary simplicity having been defined as 'enlightened material restraint' (Shi 2007: 131).

In practice, voluntary simplicity might involve growing one's own organic food, wearing second-hand clothes, riding a bike, minimising energy consumption and waste, sharing rather than buying, and working less in the formal economy in search of work/life balance and increased community engagement

(Grisby 2004). Other practices and perspectives common within the movement include: thoughtful frugality and thriftiness with respect to money; a deep respect for nature (and its limits); a desire for self-sufficiency and financial independence; a privileging of creativity and contemplation over possessions; an aesthetic preference for minimalism and functionality; and a sense of responsibility for the just uses of the world's resources (Shi 2007). Far from being about hardship or sacrifice, living simply is about living more with less. Of course, the values, perspectives, and practices of simple living are diverse, evolving, and always context-dependent.

In essence, then, voluntary simplicity is a personal and collective process of revaluing and re-contextualising the meaning and role of material consumption in the good life. It typically involves turning away from superfluous things and turning toward other sources of meaning and satisfaction that are judged to be more life enhancing and more consistent with a symbiotic relationship with nature. These practices are also shaped significantly by the structures within which we live, which is why personal action alone or a mere shift in consciousness will never be enough to achieve a sustainable world. We also need new structures and systems that support and encourage voluntary simplicity, as well as an ethical transformation that makes this new conception of flourishing not just workable but desirable.

So how might this approach to the good life relate to the steady state economy?

3. Voluntary Simplicity as the Cultural Foundation of a Steady-state Economy

It is difficult to establish precisely the size of the voluntary simplicity movement, but the largest empirical study in this area (Alexander and Ussher, 2012) has presented a case that as many as 200 million people in the developed world could be embracing lifestyles of voluntary simplicity. This study does acknowledge, however, that there will be a wide diversity of lifestyles within this large demographic, with some participants taking relatively minor steps to 'downshift' or 'simplify' and others taking more radical steps. Nevertheless, if these people are connected by their attempt to reduce or restrain their consumption – and if they also *feel* connected – then together they constitute a social movement of considerable collective power and politico-economic import, potentially, at least.

Our central point is that the voluntary simplicity movement will almost certainly need to expand, organise, radicalise, and politicise, if a degrowth or steady state economy is to emerge through democratic processes. This is the 'grassroots' or 'bottom up' theory of structural transformation that motivates our work. The essential reasoning here is that legal, political, and economic structures will never reflect a post-growth vision of macroeconomic sufficiency until a post-consumerist ethics of material sufficiency is embraced and mainstreamed at the cultural level. Conversely, the cultural embrace of a consumerist worldview will always generate, or try to generate, a macroeconomics of growth.

This may be the kind of reasoning which led Robyn Eckersley (1992: 17) to state that 'the environmental problematic is a crisis of culture and character'. Indeed, we would argue that the various problems of growth economics could be characterised in much the same way, suggesting that the fundamental causes of, and the solutions to, those problems may lie fundamentally in dominant cultural understandings of prosperity which are deeply shaped by visions of material affluence. This is not to deny, of course, that many structural changes will be a key part of any transformative steady state economics and politics; it is only to propose that such deep transformation in the legal, political, and macroeconomic spheres will ultimately depend on a broad socio-cultural consensus that deems such transformation necessary and legitimate. We suspect many and perhaps most advocates of steady state economics would sympathise with this theory of change (e.g., Daly and Cobb, 1994). We do note, however, that within the literature on steady state economics the socio-cultural analysis of consumption has been less developed to date than the economic analyses (but see the chapter on Consumption), and suggest accordingly that this is an area where steady state scholarship could be enriched by a closer engagement with the voluntary simplicity literature. Conversely, the voluntary simplicity movement has much to learn from the structural and systemic analyses of steady state economics.

4. Synergies and Divergences

There are a number of more specific synergies between voluntary simplicity and the social arrangements conducive to a steady state economy. There are also some differences and divergences, although mostly these are matters of emphasis not vision.

First, voluntary simplicity traditionally takes an individual household or 'microeconomic' perspective of the good life. Most of the literature about simple living is addressed to individuals and how they can exercise choice within the scope of their personal lifestyles and families to improve quality of life through reducing material consumption. On the other hand, steady state economics primarily (though not exclusively) offers a set of big-picture macroeconomic analyses and policy recommendations. There is often a divergence of scale between these two ways of looking at life, though certainly not a discontinuity of the values that inform both perspectives.

Both steady state economists and practitioners of voluntary simplicity care deeply about ecological limits and social justice. Both see conserving ecosystems and reducing inequity as intimately tied up with decisions about consumption. The steady state goal of limiting the scale of the economy relative to the ecosphere would be endorsed by practitioners of simple living.

Second, there is little reference in the simplicity literature to population issues. But we would suggest that among most practitioners of voluntary simplicity, limiting population as a necessary condition for a flourishing civilisation is a perspective so taken for granted that it scarcely gets mentioned. That said, recognising the challenge and knowing how to resolve it are two separate things, and given the importance of the issue we suggest that the voluntary simplicity movement ought to be more vocal and explicit about population matters.

From its earliest formulations, steady state economics has urged limits on human population as a prerequisite for attaining a steady state within Earth's carrying capacity (Daly 1995). Just how this might be achieved is a continuing topic of discussion and controversy.

Third, mindfulness practice helps us distinguish material from nonmaterial needs. As we become more skilled at securing appropriate satisfiers for each, we discover that material needs are small and relatively stable over time, thus calling for a small, steady state economy to provide for them. The emphasis in consumer culture on production for affluence derives from its tendency to conflate nonmaterial desires (which are limitless) with material consumption (which is constrained by planetary limits and individual material needs). The insights offered by voluntary simplicity about the limited role material things need to play in a full and meaningful human life, and how to cultivate mindfulness about our consumption choices, offer a powerful complement to macroeconomic policies in promoting overall sustainability and sufficiency in our economics lives.

Fourth, the history and present-day practice of voluntary simplicity illustrate that a high quality of life depends jointly on sufficient material provision and abundance of non-material experiences that contribute to wellbeing. Fortunately, sufficient material provision should be easy to achieve within ecological limits if our economy and marketing methods do not systematically and artificially inflame desire for material goods as proxies for meeting nonmaterial needs, as they do under a growth economy. Once material needs have been met, the extra ecological footprint incurred for meeting nonmaterial needs could be remarkably small if pursued thoughtfully. Practitioners of voluntary simplicity, therefore, provide living examples of the good life that would be possible in a steady state economy. At the same time, without the structures and systems of a steady state economy, living simply is much harder than it needs to be.

Fifth, living within the means of what the planet can provide, as urged by steady state economics, is likely to require a significant shift away from economic globalisation and toward increased localisation. Voluntary simplicity recognises self-reliance and community reliance as key elements of a good life. Cooperating with our neighbours to provide local goods and services contributes to community economic development, so we see that voluntary simplicity has much overlap with other movements too, like the sharing economy, transition towns, and permaculture. Such cooperation builds economic assets with tools such as local currencies, barter systems, cooperative enterprises, and all manner of production using local labour and resources. These practices also build the dense network of relationships that include, but also transcend, economic exchange relationships.

Psychological research has repeatedly shown that the quality of our relationships is the most important contributor to well-being, followed closely by the quality of our work experience, access to leisure, and physical health (for a review, see Alexander 2015: Ch 2). Beyond modest sufficiency, monetary riches occupy a distant fourth or fifth place on the list of what makes for a good life. Promoting personal and community self-reliance is highly synergistic with the requirements of a steady state economy.

5. The Analysis of Desire

Perhaps the greatest difference between the voluntary simplicity movement and steady state economics is the analysis of desire (or lack thereof). For simple living, this analysis is fundamental to a good life. The origins of desire seem to be mostly lacking from economic theory and analysis. Mainstream economics rests on an 18th-century theory of human psychology and motivation that finds little empirical support from modern psychological research (see the critique of the 'standard economic model' offered in Schor, 2009).

The mainstream or neoclassical discipline of economics

claims that people can be forced to modify the expression of their desires through their consumption behaviour. The forcing device is the pricing mechanism, which is driven by those who want to exploit desire to generate profit. But in reality, changing behaviour requires much more than getting the prices right. It requires both inquiry into the nature of desire itself and further insight or self-awareness on the part of consumers. We need to reimagine the good life beyond consumer culture (see Assadourian, 2010) and ask questions about why we desire what we desire.

Certainly people can be coerced to behave in certain ways by creating price incentives for desired behaviour. But another approach is possible that grows from enlightened self-aware-ness — not just 'rational' self-interest. Human behaviour and human societies can change when our consciousness of our-selves and our relationships change, as is demonstrated by other progressive social movements (e.g., civil rights, women's rights, gay rights, etc.). Since consciousness is at least partly socially constructed, it is through our relationships with other humans, animals, and nature that transformations of consciousness can occur. Therefore, changing the focal length of consciousness through mindfulness practice represents a post-consumerist pathway toward a better life.

There is noteworthy consistency over centuries and across cultures that the choice to adopt a simpler life is usually preceded by a fundamental change in worldview (Wagner 1903, 17). Sometimes this is caused by trauma or loss (Spina 1998), sometimes by deliberate spiritual practice (Kasser and Brown 2005), and sometimes it happens as a series of spontaneous insights that lead us to question our previous understanding of what constitutes the good life and to seek alternatives (Elgin 2010; Pierce 2000).

6. Conclusion

We see many deep synergies between a steady state economy and the sorts of policies and social structures that support simple living or voluntary simplicity. Broad acceptance of a steady state economy would appear necessarily to include the cultural practice of simple living, especially if the transition is to be democratic and involve the majority of citizens. Voluntary simplicity has much to offer in achieving a steady state economy through its analysis of material desire and its emphasis on the power of mindfulness to transform consciousness in that regard. Voluntary simplicity can also help us evolve philosophically and psychologically toward wanting what we must in any case do. Most importantly of all, perhaps, practising voluntary simplicity can help liberate them from the 'work-and-spend' cycle, thereby providing people with more time and energy to get active in their communities building the new economy from the grass-roots up. The motivating concern of this chapter was to draw more attention to what role cultural evolution toward voluntary simplicity might play in providing a key driver in the transition toward a steady state economy.

References

Alexander, S. and Ussher, S. 2012. 'The voluntary simplicity movement: A multi-national survey analysis in theoretical context', *Journal of Consumer Culture* 12(1), 66–88.

Alexander, S. 2015. *Sufficiency economy: Enough, for everyone, forever*, Simplicity Institute Publishing, Melbourne.

Assadourian, E. 2010. 'The rise and fall of consumer cultures', in WorldWatch Institute, *Transforming cultures: From consumerism to sustainability*, WorldWatch Institute, State of the World. 2010. Chapter One.

Burch, M. 2000. *Stepping lightly: Simplicity for people and planet*, New Society Publishers, Gabriola Island.

Daly, H. 1995. 'The steady-state economy: Alternative to growthmania, in *Steady State Economics* (2nd edn), Island Press, Washington DC, pp 180–194.

Daly, H. and Cobb, J. 1989. *For the common good: Redirecting the economy toward community, environment, and a sustainable future*, Beacon Press, Boston.

Eckersley, R. 1992. *Environmentalism and political theory: Toward an eccentric approach*, State University of New York, Albany.

Elgin, D. 2010. *Voluntary simplicity: Toward a way of life that is outwardly simple, inwardly rich*, 2nd edn, HarperCollins, New York.

Grigsby, M. 2004. *Buying time and getting by: The voluntary simplicity movement*, State University of New York Press, Albany.

Kasser, T. and Brown, K. 2009. 'A scientific approach to voluntary simplicity', in Andrews, C. and Urbanska, W. 2009. *Less is more: Embracing simplicity for a healthy planet, a caring economy and lasting happiness*, New Society Publishers, Gabriola Island, pp 35–40.

Pierce, L. 2000. *Choosing simplicity: Real people finding peace and fulfillment in a complex world*, Gallagher Press, Carmel.

Schor, J. 2009. 'The new politics of consumption', in Alexander, S. (ed.) *Voluntary simplicity: The poetic alternative to consumer culture*, Stead and Daughters Ltd, Wanganui, pp 253-269.

Shi, D. 2007 (revised edn). *The simple life: Plain living and high thinking in American culture*, University of Georgia Press, Athens.

Spina, A.C. 1998. 'Research shows new aspects of voluntary simplicity', The Simple Living Network On-Line Newsletter, January–March, 1999.

Trainer, T. 2010. *The transition to a sustainable and just world*, Envirobook, Sydney.

Wagner, C. 1903. *The simple life*, McClure, Philips & Co., New York.

6

FRUGAL ABUNDANCE IN AN AGE OF LIMITS: ENVISIONING A DEGROWTH SOCIETY

1. Introduction

This chapter considers whether, or to what extent, different forms of 'austerity' exist, or could exist, in relation to material standards of living. Could an austerity externally imposed be experienced very differently from an austerity voluntary embraced? The analysis seeks to show, somewhat paradoxically, perhaps, that although reduced consumption and production within existing capitalist economies tends to impact negatively on social wellbeing – representing one form of 'austerity' – reduced consumption and production within different economic frameworks, and within different value systems, could open up space for a positive, enriching form of austerity. This latter form of austerity, it will be argued, has the potential to increase social and ecological wellbeing in an age of environmental limits (Meadows *et al.*, 2004; Jackson, 2009; Turner, 2014). It is extremely important, of course, that these two austerities are not confused, and the present inquiry into the potential for enriching forms of austerity must not be interpreted as defending the neoliberal or capitalist forms of austerity being implemented in many economies today (see, e.g., Hermann, 2014; Pollin, 2013). A distinction will be made, therefore, between an austerity of degrowth – which will be the focus of this analysis – and a capitalist austerity.

Even a cursory inquiry into the definition of austerity high-lights the various ways this term can be understood. In recent years this notion has been used almost exclusively to refer to a macroeconomic policy of crisis-management provoked by the global financial crisis, where governments cut social services in an attempt to reduce budget deficits and stimulate growth (see, e.g., Ivanova, 2013). One online dictionary defines austerity as a 'severe and rigid economy', and that is certainly how many people would experience austerity under capitalism today. Note how austerity in this sense is oblivious to the limits to growth critique. Far from trying to move beyond the growth paradigm, austerity under capitalism is defended on the grounds that it will help get the engine of growth started again.

But this is a relatively new way of understanding austerity. Prior to the global financial crisis, austerity did not refer pri-marily to a strict macroeconomic policy that cut social services. Instead, online dictionary definitions also define austerity as 'simple or plain', 'not fancy', 'unadorned', or 'a situation where money is spent only on things that are necessary'. In this very different sense of austerity, the term can be understood as a synonym for frugality or simplicity of living (see Alexander and McLeod, 2014), and it is this second form of austerity that will be the focus of this chapter. It is a form of austerity that is arguably necessary in an age of limits – necessary, that is, if we are to turn current economic and environmental crises into opportunities by way of a degrowth transition (Latouche, 2009; Schneider *et al.*, 2010; Kallis, 2011).

Among other things, a degrowth transition will involve examining or re-examining what is truly necessary to live a dignified life, as well as letting go of so much of what is super-fluous and wasteful in consumer societies today (Vale and Vale, 2013; Hamilton and Denniss, 2005). A strong but perhaps counter-intuitive case can be made that the wealthiest regions of the world can get by with a far lower material standard of living and yet increase quality of life (Alexander, 2012a; Trainer, 2012; Schor, 2010; Wilkinson and Pickett, 2010), and this is the paradox of simplicity that lies at the heart of what I am calling an 'austerity of degrowth'. A degrowth economy may be 'austere' (but sufficient) in a material sense, especially in comparison to the cultures of consumption prevalent in developed regions of the world today. But such austerity could also liberate those developed or over-developed societies from the shackles of consumerist cultures (Kasser, 2002), freeing them from materialistic conceptions of the good life and opening up space for seeking prosperity in various non-materialistic forms of satisfaction and meaning.

Serge Latouche (2014) describes a degrowth society as being one of 'frugal abundance', but what would this look like and how would it be experienced in daily life? The degrowth movement to date has focused a great deal on the macroeconomic and political dimensions of 'planned economic contraction' (Alexander, 2012b), but less attention has been given to the implications such contraction would have on our lives, at the personal and community levels. Consequently, this area of neglect calls for closer examination, because it is at the personal and community levels where degrowth would be experienced, first and foremost. Indeed, an inquiry into the *lived reality* of degrowth may be one of the best ways of describing and understanding what we mean by degrowth, moving beyond vague abstractions or 'top down' macroeconomic and political perspectives. In other words, we might gain a clearer understanding of degrowth by imagining someone mending their clothes or sharing their hammer or bicycle in conditions of scarcity, than by imagining a new financial system or political framework.

Whatever the case, this chapter focuses on the former perspective and explores how an austerity of degrowth may be experienced at the personal and social levels. This inquiry follows coherently from the various arguments in favour of degrowth that have been developing in recent years, which have offered many compelling reasons *why* we should 'degrow' (see generally, Latouche, 2009; Alexander, 2012b). But it is also important to explore more closely what degrowth would actually look like and how it might be experienced. After all, if people cannot envision the degrowth alternative with sufficient clarity, and see it as desirable, it is unlikely that a large social movement will arise to bring a degrowth economy into existence.

1.1 Framing and contextualising the analysis

Before getting to the substantive analysis a few more intro-ductory comments may help better frame and contextualise the discussion. If degrowth means – among other things – a deep and rapid transition away from high-consumption lifestyles, then we could begin an inquiry into an austerity of degrowth with a question: How would the ordinary citizen in developed nations deal with an 'austere' lifestyle of radical simplicity? By radical simplicity I do not mean poverty, which is involuntary and full of suffering and anxiety, and therefore universally unde-sirable. Rather, by radical simplicity I essentially mean a very low but biophysically sufficient material standard of living. In a world of seven billion people and counting, the transition to a just and sustainable world necessarily implies consuming at far lower material and energy levels than are common in developed nations today (Trainer, 2010). One must acknowledge, however, that from within the dominant culture of consumption, giving up consumer lifestyles would be generally perceived as some-thing that would reduce wellbeing and signify a turn away from progress.

In this chapter I want to suggest that radical simplicity would not be as bad as it might first seem, provided people were ready for it and wisely negotiated its arrival, both as individuals and as communities. I am tempted to go further and suggest that radical simplicity may be exactly what consumer cultures need to shake themselves awake from their comfortable routines and habits of consumption; that radical simplicity would be in our own, immediate, self-interests (Trainer, 2012). This is a promising possibility, because it seems clear enough that in an age of gross ecological overshoot (Global Footprint Network, 2012; Vale and Vale, 2013), degrowth as a macroeconomic and political programme in wealthy nations requires and depends upon lifestyles of radically reduced consumption. But again, it must be emphasised that reduced consumption under capitalism would be very different to reduced consumption under a planned, equitable degrowth framework, in ways that I hope to explain.

It goes without saying, of course, that if a radically lower material standard of living were to be imposed upon people suddenly by force of circumstances and without anticipation and some preparation, most people would find such a dramatic change terrifying and painful – an existential disaster. Such a response would be quite natural and understandable, for many people would have their identities and worldviews shaken beyond recognition. But the subtext of this chapter is that if such dramatic lifestyle changes were to be stoically anticipated and prepared for, even embraced, people could discover that lives of reduced consumption might lead to a new form of abundance, a new form of wealth, a new connection or reconnection with nature, our communities, and, indeed, ourselves. This is the possibility, at least, that makes degrowth such a tantalising movement for deep societal transformation, for it gives rise to the possibility that there could be 'an upside to down' (Homer-Dixon, 2006; Odum and Odum, 2001).

If this understanding of degrowth is correct (see Alexander, 2012a), it would seem that high consumption cultures could benefit greatly from anticipating and preparing for radical simplicity; benefit greatly, that is, from 'prefiguring' a simpler way of life (Trainer, 2010). Consumerism and the growth paradigm that supports it have no future, a diagnosis that I will not attempt to defend here but rather take as given, the case having been made many times before (see, e.g., Meadows *et al.*, 2004; Jackson, 2009; Smith and Positano, 2010; Turner, 2014). When consumerism's time is up, we will all be living more simply, to varying degrees, whether we want to or not. So it is important that individuals, communities, and political units deal with this inevitable change positively, and embrace the changes that are likely to lie ahead of us and make the best of them. We are being challenged to make opportunities out of the crisis of capitalism, and envisioning the practical realities of this challenge is an issue that deserves increased scholarly attention.

In the following substantive sections, therefore, I attempt to describe a radical alternative economic vision, an economic vision based on notions of simplicity, frugality, moderation, sufficiency, resilience, relocalisation, and mindfulness. In the broadest terms, this form of economy would be one that has low energy and resource requirements relative to developed economies, but which sufficiently provides for local material needs using mostly local resources, without being relentlessly driven to expand by the growth-focused ethics of profit-maximisation. What would an economy based on material sufficiency look like?

It should be acknowledged that there are a huge number of important structural issues that the following analysis does not attempt to deal with in any detail. I am referring here to issues such as property rights, banking systems, urban infrastructure, political systems, and so forth. These are all important issues to consider. But the present analysis will focus primarily on some of the socio-economic implications of degrowth at the personal and household levels, briefly discussing how our relationships to water, food, clothing, housing, energy, work, money, and technology may need to evolve, on the assumption that capitalism continues to break down over coming years and decades (Bauman and Bordoni, 2014; Tverberg, 2012; Gilding, 2011), and as emerging movements try to build an alternative degrowth economy from the grassroots up (Alexander, 2013).

It should be clear that this is not an inquiry into theoretical issues, but instead an inquiry into what may be experienced as the most basic features of day-to-day life in a degrowth economy. The aim is to ground the theory as far as possible in practical considerations; to give the theoretical bones some flesh by way of an 'envisioning' exercise. The intention, to be clear, is not to prescribe a blueprint that must be mechanically imposed everywhere, but rather to provoke thought about how degrowth could be realised in various ways. If the reader disagrees with aspects of the analysis, please adapt and refine the analysis and apply it in context-appropriate ways in order to advance the discussion.

2. Envisioning an Austerity of Degrowth

2.1 Water

This envisioning exercise begins by considering water, it being an essential basic need. In most urban contexts the amount of roof space available to collect water would be insufficient to secure the necessary water supplies for such dense populations, especially in relatively dry climates or seasons. What this means is that most urban contexts *require* the water mains to exist, for if they failed for more than a day or so, most people would quickly perish. Accordingly, a degrowth economy must at least have the energy supply and stability to maintain the water mains at a sufficiently high level of regularity and safety. The water mains is the most critical piece of urban infrastructure we have, and I suspect it will be the last thing we will allow to fail. Even in a severe crisis, I think the human 'will to survive' will ensure that the water mains keeps functioning.

Nevertheless, in a degrowth economy attitudes to water consumption and collection would undergo a revolution. Today, average daily household water consumption in the United States is around 370 litres per person (Wikipedia 2014); in Australia it is around 230 litres per person (Australian Bureau of Statistics, 2014). By way of contrast, the United Nations (UNHCR, 2014) and the World Health Organization (WHO, 2013) advise that 20 litres per person, per day, is the minimum needed for the most basic subsistence requirements, which is the baseline used in refugee camps. In a degrowth economy, we could imagine that domestic water consumption might need to fall to somewhere between 50-70 litres per person, per day, which is enough to live a dignified existence without leaving much room for waste. Watering our productive gardens may increase this, but organic food production is more water efficient than industrial methods (see, e.g., Wood *et al.*, 2006), so ultimately this would save water overall.

In order to reduce water consumption from the mains,

various steps could be taken. First of all, every household would maximise its roof water collection via water tanks. People will become proficient in creating and connecting systems of water collection and reuse – learning the skills to do so, perhaps, at community 'skill sharing' workshops organised by the local Transition Town (see Hopkins, 2008). Greywater systems will become the household norm, including the use of tank water to flush the toilet. Eventually, composting toilets may be widely used in appropriate contexts, further reducing water consumption (see Jenkins, 2005).

In those times when people are required to draw from the water mains, there is much room for conservation. Being conscientious of water consumption when preparing food and cleaning dishes, and never watering (or even having) lawns, are important and easily implemented conservation strategies. Perhaps the largest savings in the domestic sphere can come from how we wash our clothes and ourselves. Clothes could be washed less often and showers could be shorter and taken less regularly. In fact, if required, cleaning occasionally with a bucket of water and some soap is perfectly adequate for cleanliness and hygiene. This may seem 'austere', but the critical point to note is that the same circumstances of radical simplicity would be experienced in totally different ways, depending on the mindset that was brought to experience. An austerity of degrowth may be perceived as a terrible hardship if governed by consumerist expectations, but no hardship at all if approached with a frame of mind shaped by notions of sufficiency. Fortunately, that mindset is within our control (Burch, 2014), even if the material circumstances we find ourselves in may not always be. As the ancient Chinese philosopher once said: 'He who knows he has enough is rich' (Vanebroeck, 1991: 116).

2.2 Food

A foundational issue for any economy is how it sources and produces its food, and this issue sits next to water on the list of essential needs. The globalised, industrial food production system currently in existence is highly unsustainable for various reasons. Not only are industrial farming techniques causing the severe and widespread erosion of nutrient-rich topsoil (which takes many hundreds of years to rejuvenate), but also the industrialised system is extremely fossil fuel-dependent (see generally, Brown, 2011). Natural gas is needed to produce commercial fertilisers, and oil is needed to produce commercial pesticides, to fuel farm machinery, and to create the plastics used in packaging. Furthermore, there are extremely long supply chains that reach all around the world and which are dependent therefore on oil for transport. In Australia, for example, a basket of food from the supermarket typically travels 70,000 kilometres from producer to consumer, if the distance each item travels is aggregated (Salleh, 2007). With respect to the UK, one study has the figure at 241,000 kilometres (Sustain, 2001). This fossil fuel dependency is highly problematic not only due to its link to climate change, but also because it may not be economically sustainable as oil continues to get more expensive (Rubin, 2009; Alexander, 2014a).

In a degrowth economy, food production may need to be highly localised, organic, and based on permaculture (Holmgren, 2002) or 'biointensive' (Jeavons, 2012) principles, in order to decarbonise industrial methods. One of the most significant, but often overlooked, implications of the transition away from industrial food production is the increased human labour needed for organic food production. The increased labour requirements arise primarily from the reduced reliance on energy-intensive, mechanised farm machinery, but organic fertiliser production and pest control are also typically more time intensive than industrialised techniques. Organic food production is entirely capable of feeding the world (United Nations, 2013; Jeavons, 2012), but to do so will require a huge increase in the provision of agricultural labour. This transition, however, will have many benefits, including reconnecting communities with the local land base upon which they depend for subsistence, and the health benefits associated with moving away from sedentary office or factory work toward the more active and outdoor work of farming (Mansen *et al.*, 2004; Tremblay *et al.*, 2010). Governments should do everything they can to support localised, organic agriculture, starting by putting a price on carbon. If they do not, grassroots movements should localise food production as best they can without state support.

To begin with, a degrowth economy should aim to maximise organic food production *within* the urban boundary. This would involve digging up lawns and turning them into productive vegetable gardens, and planting fruit trees in all available spaces. Nature strips could be cultivated; parks could be turned into small farms or community gardens; suitable roofs could become productive, herbs could grow on balconies and windowsills, and generally all food producing potential would be realised. Suburban backyards could keep chickens for eggs, and perhaps even small livestock, such as goats for milk and cheese. Animals are also a great source of manure for compost, and many permaculturalists build animals into their organic systems (Holmgren, 2002). There is also great potential for building raised garden beds on driveways, some footpaths or roads, and redundant car parks. Mushrooms could be cultivated on the shady side of the house for protein and household or neighbourhood aquaculture systems could provide urban centres with some of their fish supply.

Even in a degrowth economy, however, we can expect our urban households to 'import' various foods in various forms, if not always from around the world, then certainly from rural or peri-urban contexts. This, in fact, would be an absolute necessity in dense urban contexts, because growing space simply does not permit anywhere near strict self-sufficiency (see McCrae *et al.*, 2010). Even inspiring examples of urban agriculture, like Havana, in Cuba (see Friedrichs, 2013; Percy *et al.*, 2010), still require the importation of food – not only portions of its fruit and vegetables, but also its meat, minerals, and other foodstuffs, such as salt.

The mainly local and organic food production would also drastically change our consumption habits. Food would be eaten 'in season' in order to avoid having to import non-seasonal foods from the other side of the world. Preserving foods would be the most appropriate way to access those foods out of season. Generally, food would be unprocessed and require no disposable packaging. A robust carbon tax would significantly increase the relative price of meat (especially red meat) and consequently relative demand would reduce. This would open up huge tracts of land for human food production or 'rewilding' (Monbiot, 2013) that are currently used to produce grain for animals.

A degrowth economy would also vigilantly compost all its organic food wastes in order to supply the growing need for organic fertilisers, reducing the amount of so-called 'waste' currently sent to landfill.

2.3 Clothing

The primary function of clothing is to keep us warm, and its secondary function, at least in most societies today, is to cover nakedness. In consumer-orientated societies, however, clothing's purpose has evolved to become primarily about expressing one's identity or social status. In a degrowth economy, by way of contrast, the fashion industry may be considered a superfluous luxury and accordingly it could be amongst the first industries to disappear. Of course, people will always want to express themselves through what they wear, so 'style' would not disappear so much as evolve (see Reich, 1970). A new aesthetic of sufficiency could develop, and soon enough the social expectation to look fashionable would become a quirk of history, incomprehensible to the new generation.

In a degrowth economy, we could salvage, swap, and reuse clothing diligently, as well as get very good at sewing and mending. For the next few decades we could do this adequately by simply reusing and recycling the (over)abundance of clothing already in existence. In the future, when new clothing is eventually needed, the primary aims of production would be functionality and sustainability, not profit-maximisation strategies playing on the pernicious desire for ever-changing styles. Fabrics like nylon and polyester would be minimised as they are made from petrochemicals and are non-biodegradable. Functional, low-impact fabrics would be used instead, such as agricultural hemp, organic wool, and organic cotton.

2.4 Housing

The issue of housing is particularly difficult and complex. Sometimes well-meaning environmentalists give the impression that we can move directly, in the next few decades, to an agrarian village scenario where everyone is living in self-built cob houses. The fact is, however, that over the next few critical decades, most people are going to find themselves living in an urban environment that already exists – suburbia. In other words, the houses and apartment blocks that already exist now, in most cases, will remain over coming decades, no matter how inadequate they are from an ecological perspective.

Given this reality, the immediate task is making best use of existing infrastructure. David Holmgren (2012) calls this 'retrofitting the suburbs for the energy descent future'. This might involve things like taking in boarders, co-housing, or putting a caravan in the driveway to help resist further urban sprawl, or putting up curtains and sealing gaps in windows and doors to increase energy efficiency. Of course, much of the existing housing stock is poorly designed so there are real limits to what retrofitting can achieve. But much can be done, no doubt, to improve the ecological performance of existing housing (see, e.g., Mobbs, 2010).

In the long term, more people and communities would take part in the construction of their own homes to reduce costs. To limit the resources required, as well as limit the spaces needed to heat and cool, houses would be much smaller and more densely inhabited than is typically the case today. But they would be sufficient. Degrowth is about knowing how much is 'enough'.

2.5 Energy

In terms of energy use, the contrast between a growth economy and a degrowth economy could hardly be starker. Whereas growth-based industrial economies seek as much energy as possible at the lowest market price (see generally, Moriarty and Honnery, 2011), a degrowth economy would require only enough energy to provide a modest but sufficient material standard of living for all (Alexander, 2012c). This means much lower energy requirements than is common in the developed world, supplied primarily through renewable sources, although the exact levels cannot be known with any precision and are likely to be context-dependent (see Heinberg, 2011). Renewable energy sources should not be relied on to sustain an energy-intensive, growth orientated society (Honnery and Moriarty, 2012; Trainer, 2013a; Trainer, 2013b), and even if they could, we should not want this (Smith and Positano, 2010). A society based primarily on renewable energy is a low-to-moderate energy society.

These reductions in energy would inevitably imply significantly reduced production and consumption (Ayres and Warr, 2009; Hall and Klitgaard, 2010; Murphy and Hall, 2011; Murphy, 2014) – that is, would imply degrowth. This would not necessarily be a problem, however, because as has already been made clear, consumption levels in a degrowth economy would be considerably lower than in consumer societies today, thus requiring much less energy to support them (see Odum and Odum, 2001). As well as economic contraction, efficiency improvements and conservation efforts would also lessen the energy requirements of a degrowth economy. That said, 'efficiency' measures would have to be subordinate to a more fundamental ethics of 'sufficiency', in order to avoid the 'rebound effect' (Princen, 2005; Polimeni et al., 2009; Alexander, 2014b).

2.6 Transport

In a degrowth economy major reductions in transport energy may need to be achieved through the relocalisation of economies (De Young and Princen, 2012). As many parts of the global economy get suffocated from expensive oil, or reshaped through carbon taxes (Alexander, 2014a), local producers may regain the competitive advantage (Rubin, 2009). Many things once imported from all around the world will now be able to be produced more economically at the local level, although presumably some global trade will remain, only far less of it (Trainer, 2010).

Energy savings achieved through relocalisation especially applies to food production. As already noted, industrial food systems are highly dependent on oil not only for transport, but also for things like pesticides and plastic packaging. When the costs of oil increase, and if a robust carbon tax is introduced, these methods may no longer be affordable or economic. The consequence will be more localised, organic food production, and therefore vastly reduced energy requirements for transport and production. Some of the imported food for cities could be transported from farms lying on the periphery of urban contexts, using electric trains.

The other area of major energy savings in the transport sector, as implied above, relates to driving cars. In order to decarbonise the economy, people will need to drive much less, or not at all (Moriarty and Honnery, 2008). Electric cars will not be able to escape this imperative, because producing them depends on fossil fuels, and also for most people electric cars remain unaffordable. Just as importantly, it would take several decades to replace the one billion petroleum-powered vehicles on the roads today with electric vehicles, and we do not have that much time to mitigate the effects of peak oil and climate change (Anderson and Bows, 2011; Alexander, 2014a).

The only solution is driving less. Various Australian studies have reported that the median distance travelled in a car is less than 5 kilometres (Department of Transport, 2009: 4), and around one third are less than 3 kilometres (BTRE, 2002: 43). In many cases those relatively short trips could be replaced with walking, cycling, or public transport. In order to make these options viable governments may need to invest heavily in a good system of electricity-powered public transport, such as light trains or trams, as well as networks of safe bike lanes.[1] Putting a price on carbon will also provide appropriate economic incentives to reduce car dependence. When necessary, carpooling should be practised.

In the longer term, however, the most significant reductions in car dependence will result from economic relocalisation. If this transformation were to occur, driving would be unnecessary for many people, as their place of work would be either at home or reachable on a bicycle. Longer distances would generally be covered by public transport.

2.7 Work and production

In a degrowth economy, the most significant changes to work and production, noted immediately above, is that the household would once again become a place of production, not merely a place of consumption. Rather than hiring other people to grow our food, cook our meals, make our clothes, build our furniture, look after our children, maintain our houses, etc., we would generally take care of such things ourselves, so far as it were possible (Astyk, 2012). Furthermore, households would sometimes produce goods for trade or barter, such as furniture, crockery, clothes, or food, and thereby contribute to the broader local economy. Artisans might also produce speciality goods at

---

1. There are, however, deep structural complications underlying the requirement to stop driving so much, which should not be ignored. For many people today driving is the only way of getting to work, so the injunction to 'get out of your car' may frustrate those people who would love to drive less but cannot, due to a lack of viable alternatives. Suburbia was built on the basis of cheap oil, which meant that 'sprawl' was not seen as much of a problem. But now that oil is getting more expensive (Alexander, 2014b) and the climate crisis is intensifying (Anderson and Bows, 2011), the long commutes are becoming increasingly problematic, not only from a cost perspective, but also from an environmental perspective.

the household level, such as musical instruments, paintings, or various tools.

Nevertheless, a degrowth economy should not be understood to mean strict self-sufficiency at the household level. It would still be desirable for much production to take place beyond the household, but the nature of what would be produced and the values motivating production would need to be very different. The provision of basic needs – such as food, clothing, shelter, tools, and medicine – would be the primary focus of production, and the motivation would be to produce what was necessary and sufficient for a good life, rather than to produce luxuries or superfluous abundance. While some large factories would no doubt remain in order to provide certain materials or hi-tech equipment, small private businesses and worker cooperatives would in most cases replace the mega-corporation, with the local grocer and hardware store returning to Mainstreet, and community-owned-and-operated farms providing much of the community's sustenance (Hopkins, 2008; Hopkins, 2013).

The greatly reduced level of production and consumption in a degrowth economy would allow for reduced working hours for most people, at least in the formal/cash economy. This would create far more time for leisure and the necessary home production.

2.8 Money, markets, and exchange

The question of what role money, markets, and exchange would play in a degrowth economy is also complex, and cannot be fully addressed here. Nevertheless, some broad comments can be made on these subjects.

First of all, it is worth noting that throughout history, human beings have exchanged goods and services with each other, either by way of barter, gift, or through the use of money. These practices are going to continue although the nature of money, markets, and exchange will have to evolve greatly, as will our attitudes toward them. It is likely that there will still need to be 'markets' for various goods that cannot be produced within the household, and money will likely remain as the most convenient tool for 'keeping accounts', so to speak. But non-monetary forms of exchange, such as gift and barter, are likely to become much more prominent modes of economic activity (Nelson and Timmerman, 2011). Since profit-maximisation would not be the aim of market activity in a degrowth economy, less attention would be given to producing things that fetch the highest price, and more attention would be given to producing what the community most needs.

The fact that markets of some variety would probably still remain in a degrowth economy implies that some forms of private property are likely to endure, although it is just as likely, and desirable, that more of the economy comes under local democratic control (Trainer, 2010). Although the balance between private and social control of the economy could unfold in an infinite variety of ways (Alexander, 2011) – a decision that will rightly be left to each democratic community – a degrowth economy must be designed so that everyone has enough, and this means taking eco-socialistic (Sarkar, 1999) responsibility for ensuring that the basic needs of all are universally met. This will require a significant degree of social democratic control of the economy, as basic needs would not be adequately met if resource allocation were left to market forces. The most important issue would be that everyone had access to land and affordable housing, and communities might have to experiment with how best to ensure this occurred.

With respect to existing monetary systems, one of the greatest problems is that money is currently loaned into existence as debt that accrues interest, and for such systems to function they require economic growth in order for the debts *plus* the interest to be paid back (Sorrell, 2010). Interest payments imply an expansion of the money supply. A degrowth economy could not by definition have a monetary system that required growth, so it follows that interest-bearing loans could not be the primary means of money creation in such an economy (Trainer, 2011). But what should replace this debt-based system – and how the transition beyond such a system would play out – are open questions that have not received the attention they deserve (but see: Douthwaite, 2012; Kallis, Kerschner, and Martinez-Alier, 2012).

2.9 Technology

In a degrowth economy, many technological conveniences we know today may largely disappear. Microwaves, vacuum cleaners, dishwashers, electronic kitchen gadgets, etc., may all become relics of history, but without causing much hardship at all. We survived without them not so long ago. But degrowth is not 'anti-technology'. Rather, it is a position that advocates a critical consideration of 'appropriate technology' (Schumacher, 1989 [1973]; Latouche, 2014).

We should also remember, however, that a degrowth economy will likely emerge only in the wake of industrial civilisation's deterioration. This will mean that vast quantities of industrially produced goods, tools, and materials will already be in existence, and for many decades, perhaps centuries, we would be living in what some have called the 'salvage economy' (Greer, 2009). Human beings will doubtless prove to be exceedingly creative in the use and reuse of existing materials and technologies. The old ethics of the depression era may return, as people learn to 'use it up, wear it out, make it do, or do without'.

The clothesline could replace the clothes dryer; the bike will largely replace the car; and the television might essentially disappear, because we will have so many more important things to be doing. I suspect that washing machines and fridges will be the last things we give up, but life would go on even if they became unavailable or unaffordable. Hopefully computers will remain to do some important tasks – sharing important information and facilitating social organisation – although private computers might become much less common.

There are countless other avenues that this analysis could explore: what would become of existing health and education systems, or pension schemes? How would people spend their leisure time? How would a degrowth economy differ in urban centres as opposed to rural settings? And how would degrowth in the global North affect the global South? These are all issues that deserve further attention, but they go beyond the scope of the present analysis.

3. Conclusion

It will have become clear that the degrowth economy, as I have envisioned it, implies a fundamentally different way of life for most people in consumer societies today. While this way of life may seem 'austere' in material terms compared to the high-consumption lifestyles widely celebrated in consumer cultures today, the aim has been to describe a standard of living that is low but nevertheless *sufficient* to live a rich and fulfilling life (Trainer, 2012; Alexander, 2012a). In accordance with the ethics of voluntary simplicity (Cafaro and Gambel, 2009; Alexander, 2009), the essential living strategy would involve aiming to meet basic material needs in low-impact ways, then redirecting energy and attention away from limitless materialistic pursuits, in favour of seeking the 'good life' in various non-materialistic sources of satisfaction and meaning. This is the austerity of degrowth explored in this chapter.

This raises the question of how we could transition to such an economy – a question that is obviously of the highest importance (see Alexander and Rutherford, 2014). Could the transition be voted in through the parliamentary mechanisms of representative democracy? Would it require a political revolution and the introduction of some form of eco-socialism? Or would it require grassroots movements to essentially do it mostly themselves, building the new economy underneath the existing economy, without state assistance (and perhaps a lot of resistance)? My own view is that it would be unwise, at this stage, to commit unconditionally to any one strategy, given that the future is so uncertain. Different contexts may also call for differing strategies for change.

I do think, however, that the Transition Towns Movement, while not homogenous in its approach, currently has something of the right strategic balance here (Hopkins, 2008; Hopkins, 2013). Adopting what can be called 'participatory democracy', the movement basically accepts that change must be driven at the grassroots, community level, while at the same time being prepared to press on governments (mainly local governments) to assist in the transition whenever that seems to be a good use of limited energies.

Furthermore, if the Transition Movement were ever to succeed in achieving its ambitious and diverse goals, I believe something resembling a degrowth economy may well be the result. What is important, I think, is that the debate gets drawn away from the question of how to *maintain* the existing system, toward the urgent and necessary question of what system should *replace* the existing system. In this sense the humble notion of degrowth can be seen as the revolutionary, but also necessary, proposal that it is.

Degrowth is about moving toward a society of frugal abundance, a society that is not degraded by capitalist austerity in times of crisis, but enriched by an austerity of degrowth based on an ethics of voluntary simplicity. Admittedly, this analysis may have raised as many questions as it has answered, but it is hoped that the exercise of envisioning a degrowth economy at the socio-economic levels helps advance the debate around this necessary movement for deep and rapid societal change.

References

Alexander, S. (ed.). 2009. *Voluntary simplicity: The poetic alternative to consumer culture*, Stead and Daughters, Whanganui.

Alexander, S. 2011. 'Property beyond growth: Toward a politics of voluntary simplicity', doctoral thesis, Melbourne Law School, available at:http://papers.ssrn.com/sol3/papers.cfm?abstract_id=1941069 (accessed 10 September, 2013).

Alexander, S. 2012a. 'The optimal material threshold: Toward an economics of sufficiency', *Real-World Economics Review* 61, pp 2–21.

Alexander, S. 2012b. 'Planned economic contraction: The emerging case for degrowth', *Environmental Politics* 21 (3), pp 349–368.

Alexander, S. 2012c. 'Degrowth, expensive oil, and the new economics of energy', *Real-World Economics Review* 61, pp 40–51.

Alexander, S. 2013. 'Voluntary simplicity and the social reconstruction of law: Degrowth from the grassroots up', *Environmental Values* 22 (2), pp 287–308.

Alexander, S. 2014a. 'The new economics of oil', *MSSI Issues Paper* (No. 2, March 2014), pp 1–15.

Alexander, S. 2014b. 'A critique of techno-optimism: Efficiency without sufficiency is lost', *MSSI Working Paper* (WP 1/14), pp 1–21.

Alexander, S. and McLeod, A. 2014. *Simple living in history: Pioneers of the deep future*, Simplicity Institute Publishing, Melbourne.

Alexander, S. and Rutherford, J. 2014. 'The deep green alternative: Debating strategies of transition', *Simplicity Institute Report* 14a, pp 1–24.

Anderson, K. and Bows, A. 2011. 'Beyond "dangerous" climate change: Emissions scenarios for a new world', *Philosophical Transitions of the Royal Society* 369, pp 3863–3882.

Astyk, S. 2012. *Making home: Adapting our homes and our lives to settle in place*, New Society Publishers, Gabriola Island.

Australian Bureau of Statistics. 2014. 'Water Account, Australia, 2009-10', available at: http://www.abs.gov.au/ausstats/abs@.nsf/Lookup/CAE301277A675941CA257956000E646E?opendocument (accessed 2 November 2014).

Ayres, R. and Warr, B. 2009. *The economic growth engine: How energy and work drive material prosperity*, Edward Elgar, Cheltenham, UK.

Bauman, Z. and Bordoni, C. 2014. *State of Crisis*, Polity Press, Cambridge.

Brown, L. 2011. *World on the edge: How to prevent environmental and economic collapse*, W.W. Norton and Co., New York.

BTRE (Bureau of Transport and Regional Economics). 2002. 'Greenhouse policy options for transport', available at: http://www.bitre.gov.au/

publications/2002/files/report_105.pdf (accessed 2 November 2014).

Burch, M. 2013. *The hidden door: Mindful sufficiency as an alternative to extinction*, Simplicity Institute Publishing, Melbourne.

Cafaro, P. and Gambrel, J. 2009. 'The virtue of simplicity', *Journal of Agricultural and Environmental Ethics* 23 (1), p. 85.

De Gues, M. 1999. *Ecological utopias: Envisioning the sustainable society*, International Books, Utrecht.

Department of Transport. 2009. 'Victorian Integrated Survey of Travel and Activity 2007', available at: http://www.transport.vic.gov.au/__ data/assets/pdf_file/0014/31280/VISTA-07-Summary-Brochure.pdf (accessed 2 November 2014).

De Young, R. and Princen, T. (eds). 2012. *The localization reader: Adapting to the coming downshift*, MIT Press, Cambridge.

Douthwaite, R. 2012. 'Degrowth and the supply of money in an energy-constrained world', *Ecological Economics* 84, pp 187–193.

Friedrichs, J. 2013. *The future is not what it used to be: Climate change and energy scarcity*, MIT Press, Cambridge, MA.

Gilding, P. 2011. *The great disruption: How the climate crisis will transform the global economy*, Bloomsbury, London.

Global Footprint Network., 2013. Resources available at: http://www. footprintnetwork.org/en/index.php/GFN/page/annual_report/ (accessed 29 October 2013).

Greer, J.M. 2009. *The ecotechnic future: Envisioning a post-peak world*, New Society Publishers, Gabriola Island.

Hall, C. and Klitgaard, K. 2012. *Energy and the wealth of nations: Understanding the biophysical economy*, Springer, New York.

Hamilton, C. and Denniss, R. 2005. *Affluenza: When too much is never enough*, Allen & Unwin, Crows Nest, NSW.

Heinberg, R. 2011. *The end of growth: Adapting to our new economic reality*, New Society Publishers, Gabriola Island.

Hermann, C. 2014. 'Structural adjustment and neoliberal convergence in labour markets and welfare: The impact of the crisis and austerity measures on European economics and social models', *Competition and Change* 18 (2), pp 111–130.

Holmgren, D. 2002. *Permaculture: Principles and pathways beyond sustainability*, Holmgren Design Services, Hepburn.

Holmgren, D. 2012. 'Retrofitting the suburbs for the energy descent future', *Simplicity Institute Report* 12i, pp 1–8.

Homer-Dixon, T. 2006. *The upside of down: Catastrophe, creativity, and the renewal of civilisation*, Island Press, Washington.

Hopkins, R. 2008. *The transition handbook: From oil dependency to local resilience*, Chelsea Green Publishing, White River Junction, Vt.

Hopkins, R. 2013. *The power of just doing stuff*, Green Books, UIT Cambridge, Cambridge.

Ivanova, M. 'The Great Recession and the state of American capitalism', *Science and Society* 77 (3), pp 294–314.

Jackson, T. 2009. *Prosperity without growth: Economics for a finite planet*, Earthscan, London.

Jeavons, J. 2012 (8th edn). *How to grow more vegetables*, Ten Speed Press, Berkeley.

Jenkins, J. 2005 (3rd edn). *The humanure handbook: A guide to composting human manure*, Chelsea Green Publishing, White River Junction, VT.

Kallis, G. 2011. 'In defence of degrowth', *Ecological Economics* 70, pp 873–80.

Kallis, G., Kerschner, C., and Martinez-Alier, J. 2012. 'The economics of degrowth', *Ecological Economics* 84, pp 172–180.

Kasser, T. *The high price of materialism*, MIT Press, Cambridge, MA.

Latouche, S. 2009. *Farewell to growth*, Polity Press, Cambridge, UK.

Latouche, S. 2014. 'Essays on frugal abundance (1 of 4) – Degrowth: misunderstandings and controversies', *Simplicity Institute Report* 14c, pp 1–22.

MacRae, R. *et al.* 2010. 'Could Toronto provide 10% of its fresh vegetable requirements from within its own boundaries? Matching consumption requirements with growing space', *Journal of Agriculture, Food Systems, and Community Development* 1 (2), pp 105-127.

Meadows, D., Randers, J., and Meadows, D. 2004. *Limits to growth: The 30-year update*, Chelsea Green Publishing, White River Junction, Vt.

Monbiot, G. 2013. *Feral: Searching for enchantment on the frontiers of rewilding*, Penguin, London.

Moriarty, P. and Honnery, D. 2008. 'Low-mobility: The future of transport', *Futures* 40, pp 865–872.

Moriarty, P. and Honnery, D. 2011. *Rise and fall of the carbon civilisation: Resolving global environmental and resource problems*, Springer-Verlag, London.

Moriarty, P. and Honnery, D. 2012. 'What is the global potential for renewable energy?', *Renewable and Sustainable Energy Reviews* 16 (1), pp 244–252.

Murphy, D. 2014. 'The implications of the declining energy return on investment of oil production', *Philosophical Transactions of the Royal Society* A, 372, 20130126, pp 1–19.

Murphy, D. and Hall, C. 2011. 'Energy return on investment, peak oil, and the end of economic growth', *Annals of the New York Academy of Sciences* 1219, pp 52–72.

Odum, E. and Odum, H. 2001. *A prosperous way down: Principles and policies*, University Press of Colorado, Colorado.

Percy, E. *et al.* 2010. 'Planning for peak oil: Learning from Cuba's "Special Period"', *Urban Design and Planning* 163(4), p. 169.

Pollin, R. 2013. 'Austerity economics and the struggle for the soul of US capitalism', *Social Research* 80 (3), pp 749–780.

Princen, T. 2005. *The logic of sufficiency*, MIT Press, Cambridge, MA.

Polimeni, J. *et al.* 2009. *The myth of resource efficiency: The Jevons paradox*, Earthscan, London.

Mansen, J., Skerrett, P., Greenland, P., and VanItallie, T. 2004. 'The escalating pandemics of obesity and sedentary lifestyle: A call to action for clinicians', *Archives of Internal Medicine* 164(3), pp 249–258.

Mobbs, M. 2010 (2nd edn). *Sustainable house*, UNSW Press, Sydney.

Nelson, A. and Timmerman, F. 2011. *Life without money: Building fair and sustainable economies*, Pluto Press, London.

Reich, C. 1970. *The greening of America*, Crown Trade Paperbacks, New York.

Rubin, J. 2009. *Why your world is about to get a whole lot smaller*, Virgin, London.

Salleh, A. 2007. 'Food miles can mislead', ABC Science, available at: http://www.abc.net.au/science/articles/2007/11/28/2103395.htm (accessed 10 January 2012).

Sarkar, S. 1999. *Eco-socialism or eco-capitalism: A critical analysis of humanity's fundamental choices*, Zed books, London.

Schneider, F., Kallis, G., and Martinez-Alier, J. 2010. 'Crisis or opportunity? Economic degrowth for social equity and ecological sustainability', *Journal of Clean Production*, 18(6), pp 511–518.

Schor, J. 2010. *Plenitude: The new economics of true wealth*, Penguin Press, New York.

Schumacher, E. 1989 [1973]. *Small is beautiful: Economics as if people mattered*, Harper Perennial, New York.

Smith, J. and Positano, S. 2010. *The self-destructive affluence of the first world: The coming crises of global poverty and ecological collapse*, Edwin Mellen, New York.

Sorrell, S. 2010. 'Energy, economic growth, and environmental sustainability: Five propositions', *Sustainability* 2 (6), pp 1784–1809.

Sustain, 2001. 'Eating oil – food in a changing climate', *A Sustain / Elm Farm Research Centre Report*, available at: http://www.sustainweb.org/pdf/eatoil_sumary.PDF (accessed 10 March, 2014).

Trainer, T. 2010. *The transition to a sustainable and just world*, Envirobook, Sydney.

Trainer, T. 2011. 'The radical implications of zero growth economy',

Real-World Economics Review 57, pp 71–82.

Trainer, T. 2012. 'Your delightful day: The benefits of life in The Simpler Way', *Simplicity Institute Report* 13b, pp 1–8.

Trainer, T. 2013a. 'Can Europe run on renewable energy? A negative case', *Energy Policy* 63, pp 845–850.

Trainer, T. 2013b. 'Can the world run on renewable energy', *Humanomics* 29 (2), pp 88–104.

Tremblay, M., Colley, R., Saunders, T., Healy, G., and Owen, N. 2010. 'Physiological and health implications of a sedentary lifestyle', *Applied Physiology, Nutrition, and Metabolism* 35, pp 725–740.

Turner, G. 2014. 'Is collapse imminent? An updated comparison of the *Limits to Growth* with historical data', *MSSI Research Paper* (No.4, August 2014), pp 1–21.

Tverberg, G. 2012. 'Oil supply limits and the continuing financial crisis', *Energy* 37 (1), pp 27–34.

United Nations. 2013. 'Wake up before it's too late: Make agriculture truly sustainable now for food security in a changing climate', *Trade and Environment Review* 2013, available at: http://unctad.org/en/ PublicationsLibrary/ditcted2012d3_en.pdf

UNHCR. 2014. 'Water, Sanitation and Hygiene', available at: http://www. unhcr.org/pages/49c3646cef.html (accessed 2 November 2014).

Vale, R. and Vale, B. 2013. *Living within a fair share ecological footprint*, Earthscan, London.

Vanenbroeck, G. (ed.). 1991. *Less is more: An anthology of ancient and modern voices raised in praise of simplicity*, Inner Traditions, Vermont.

Wikipedia. 2014. 'Water supply and sanitation in the United States', available at: http://en.wikipedia.org/wiki/Water_supply_and_sani- tation_in_the_United_States (accessed 2 November 2014).

Wilkinson, R. and Pickett, K. 2010. *The spirit level: Why greater equality makes societies stronger*, Penguin, London.

Wood, R., Lenzen, M., Dey, C., and Lundie, S. 2006. 'A comparative study of some environmental impacts of conventional and organic farming in Australia', *Agricultural Studies* 89 (2-3), pp 324–348.

World Health Organization. 2013. 'How much water is needed in emer- gencies?', available at: http://www.who.int/water_sanitation_health/ publications/2011/WHO_TN_09_How_much_water_is_needed. pdf?ua=1 (accessed 2 November 2014).

7

WILD DEMOCRACY: A BIODIVERSITY OF RESISTANCE AND RENEWAL

1. Introduction

With characteristic insight, the great American philosopher John Dewey once wrote: 'Every generation has to accomplish democracy over again for itself' (Dewey, 1981-90: 299). His point was that, at each moment in history, citizens and nations inevitably face unique challenges and problems, so we should not assume the democratic institutions and practices inherited from the past will be adequate for the conditions of today. Our ongoing political challenge, therefore, is to 'accomplish' democracy anew, every generation.

It seems we have forgotten Dewey's lesson. Too often we assume instead that democracy is something that has been achieved already, once and for all. Why do we need to reinvent it? Indeed, in the wake of a recent federal election (in Australia), it is easy to be seduced back to the comfortable unfreedom of the shopping mall or withdraw into the existential numbness of social media or television, believing that, having voted, our political work is done. The task of governing is now in the hands of our so-called 'representatives'. That's what political participation means in a market capitalist society, doesn't it?

This is, of course, an impoverished, even dangerous, conception of democracy, which we propagate by way of casual apathy at our own peril. It is government *of* the people, certainly, but not government *by* the people and increasingly not *for* the people. Accordingly, with a deferential nod to Dewey, below I offer an outline of a new political orientation, sensibility, and practice – a position I call 'wild democracy'. In a global tide that seems to be drifting enthusiastically toward ecocide and fascism, wild democracy signifies a radical and participatory eco-egalitarian politics that seeks to take root beyond the tired parliamentary distinctions of Left and Right, but also beyond (and yet between) the antagonistic but enriching poles of anarchism and Marxism. As I will explain, wild democracy is a localised politics with a global perspective, positioning itself 'in the wild' beyond the state and yet, at times, pragmatically engaged with the state. In short, wild democracy is a revolutionary politics without a Revolution, as such – a paradox I will unpack and defend below.[1]

1.1. Is this even a coherent theoretical project?

Readers would be right to suspect that the project indeed risks incoherency. I hope to show, however, that by drawing on the resources of both anarchism and Marxism, without adopting the encrusted ideologies of either, wild democracy has the potential to highlight deep allegiances between these rich and necessary schools of radical politics, enriching democratic practice without degenerating into theoretical incoherency.

Indeed, I will argue that the prospective allegiances become especially apparent when both anarchism and Marxism are infused with a deep green environmentalism that, first, recognises the reality of severe environmental limits to growth, and,

---

1. Although the focus of this essay is on how individuals and communities might best contribute to democratic (self)governance in today's world, there is a broader crisis of democracy underpinning this inquiry, including the deepening attacks on freedom of assembly, concentration of media, corporate influence on governments, increasing surveillance, etc. Those broader concerns about contemporary democracy provide a backdrop to the analysis but space does not permit a detailed examination as such. I acknowledge also that there is vast literature exploring, critiquing, and attempting to radicalise democracy. Rather than attempt to review existing literature, however, this essay focuses instead on presenting a line of argument in the simplest terms possible.

second, appreciates the radical implications of those limits to growth on any coherent conception of a just and sustainable society. The framing question is: how can seven billion people (and counting) live sustainably on our fragile planet? The framing answer is: surely not by globalising consumer lifestyles via continuous global economic growth. More than anything else, it is this 'limits to growth' (Meadows *et al.*, 2004) perspective that demands a contemporary re-evaluation of traditional political and economic ideologies and strategies, and this re-evaluation, I will argue, demands that we reinvent democracy – that we 'rewild' democracy in order to 'accomplish' democracy.

To state one of my key perspectives upfront: the open and often fierce conflict between anarchists and Marxists – a conflict that is now nearly two centuries old – has been, to my mind, one of the greatest shortcomings of both camps, and continues to be an obstacle on the path to change (see Newman, 2010: Ch. 3). While I do not wish to deny that there have been moments of solidarity between these camps, it would be fair to say such moments have been the exception rather than the rule. At its most ambitious, the following analysis seeks to resolve that conflict, or, less boldly, to *accommodate it* or at least *defer it*. By creating space for potential alliances between these antagonistic and often opposing schools of radical politics, the project of wild democracy represents a strategic re-evaluation of political strategy and outlook, which, if it were able to unite the diversity of radical imaginations, has the potential to engender collaborative activism and thereby advance the causes of justice and sustainability. However, that first requires a coherent exposition or unveiling of those hidden political allegiances, which is the purpose of this work-in-progress.

I acknowledge at once, of course, that there will forever be an *irresolvable* conflict between classical anarchists (e.g., Bakunin, Proudhon, Kropotkin, etc.), who categorically reject the instrument of the state, and conventional Marxists, who regard the state as a necessary instrument for the proletariat to wield on the path to the communist utopia. Nevertheless, I will maintain that *here and now* – which is the most important geographical moment in politics – there is so much groundwork to be done establishing a politically engaged post-capitalist consciousness that the disagreements between revolutionary imaginations are less important than the agreements. I will argue that it is strategically flawed for radical movements to expend time and energy fighting amongst themselves when what is needed more than anything is a united opposition to the existing reality of dehumanising and unsustainable capitalism. In short, let there be one 'no' and many 'yeses'.

The essence of my argument, then, is that our new collective goal – that is, the goal of eco-anarchists, eco-socialists, and even what might be called 'radical reformers' – should be to work collaboratively, not so much to establish our diverse and no doubt incommensurable utopias, but simply to resist, transcend, and transform the destructive capitalist dystopia that lies in the way of *any* ecozoic or humane political economy. That is the unambitious ambition of the following political analysis: not to achieve utopia but simply to transcend dystopia – which, of course, is quite ambitious enough. But, as will be seen, transcending dystopia is not intended to mean simply living in *deconstructive resistance* to the status quo. First and foremost, it also means living in the utopian spirit of *creative renewal* – prefiguring alternative, post-capitalist modes of existence – even if at first they are always and necessarily partial, compromised, temporary, and small-scale. Whether engaging in acts of resistance or renewal, the wild imagination is the most potent force at the disposal of post-capitalist social movements. The path beyond is, as yet, unimagined. This is the democracy 'to come' (see Derrida, 2010, pp 73–83).

One final note of justification: I was driven to formulate this deep green or 'ecozoic' politics of wild democracy due to the inadequacies of inherited political categories and distinctions, which left me unable to orientate myself in the space of existing political theory and practice. I did not know where I stood, because nowhere seemed quite right. Perhaps some readers similarly dissatisfied with the crude tripartite division of liberal parliamentary democracy, Marxism, and anarchism, might appreciate this 'opening up' of a more nuanced political space in a way that better reflects the intricacies of political existence in our own times. In this most preliminary statement, I put forward wild democracy as a political tool that might help carve out such a space.

2. Reinventing Democracy in the Anthropocene

In recent years the term 'Anthropocene' has entered the vocabulary of scientists and philosophers, and is slowly filtering into public discourse more broadly. In a sentence, this notion reflects the idea that human activity is now so fundamentally degrading the ecosystems of Earth that this constitutes nothing less than a new geological era – the first geological era 'caused' by humans.

Like reckless gods, we are transforming the face of Gaia, a license apparently granted to humanity (or parts of humanity) under the name of 'freedom', by the philosophy of political liberalism. Today it is widely assumed that it would be 'illiberal' to govern in such a way that would curtail ecocide. Such governance would interfere illegitimately with our so-called freedoms – our apparent human right to commit ecocide. 'Freedom for whom?' we might fairly ask.

Is it not reasonable to think that we might need to rethink politics, especially liberal democratic politics, in and for the Anthropocene? This is especially so, I would argue, given that the nations making the heaviest and most unsustainable demands on the planet are the hyper-consuming capitalist economies of the democratic West.

And yet, despite the fact that humanity is colliding dangerously with environmental limits, even the richest nations, including Australia, remain firmly entrenched in a growth paradigm that is the root cause of the ecological predicament. This state of affairs is partly driven by consumerist cultures that demand ever-rising levels of affluence, but, more insidiously, there are also various structures and vested interests within capitalism that lock us on to the treadmill of growth, influencing political decision-making in undemocratic ways. For example, the fear or threat of 'capital flight' in a globalised economy means that corporate interests shape domestic politics in ways that benefit capital and marginalise any non-capitalistic interests. The concentration of privatised mass media also bestows an undemocratic influence on a few mega-rich elites. These and many other influences of capital on democracy are diverse and powerful, and often go unnoticed. The consequence is that the cold logic of profit-maximisation maintains hegemony, as if it were the 'natural' order of things, beyond question. Business as usual more or less prevails.

Whatever the drivers of growth may be, it is perfectly clear that political parties across the spectrum today are unquestioningly committed to maintaining the growth economy, seemingly oblivious to the catastrophe that this out-dated development agenda holds in store for people and planet – a catastrophe that, in some respects, has already arrived. In short, a universal 'growth fetish' defines representative democracies today, essentially enforced by a crude liberalism that presumes interference in the so-called free market is illegitimate. Regulatory tinkering, at most, is permitted. Empire marches on.

A worrying aspect of this political blindness and paralysis is that it may be built into the very structure of representative democracies. Unable or unwilling to look beyond the short-term horizon of the next election, politicians are essentially prohibited from taking a geological view of things, which is necessary for the preservation of our biosphere. To avoid making hard decisions, environmental costs are pushed into the future, all glossed over by a techno-optimism that promises ecological salvation through technology, innovation, design, and market mechanisms. From this perspective, there is no need to question affluent lifestyles or conventional modes of development. One consequence of this non-confronting myth is that the voices of future generations fall on deaf political ears – rendering our democracy decidedly 'unrepresentative' in this glaring way.

In this context, democracy as we know it today seems to be a deeply flawed – or, at least, grossly incomplete – mode of political organisation and practice, unable to deal with the defining challenges of our times. For those people who are uncomfortably aware that limitless growth is a recipe for ecological (and thus humanitarian) disaster, the idea of trusting our growth-orientated 'representatives' to lead the way to a just and sustainable economy seems a delusion too large to swallow. Like Kafka, we will be waiting a long time.

Furthermore, one only needs to watch a single session of 'question time' in parliament to become convinced beyond doubt that democratic debate today has degenerated into shallow, often juvenile, power-hungry bickering, expressed in simplistic sound bites – a televised manifestation of 'fiddling while Rome burns'. It tempts one to despair. Certainly, one has to turn away.

Accordingly, wild democracy begins with the premise that the 'normal' party politics of representative democracy lies, for the foreseeable future, at least, beyond hope and redemption. Voting cannot possibly complete our civic duty, because our range of representatives is depressingly limited – Shorten or Turnbull? Clinton or Trump? – a political 'Sophie's choice'. Whether we look to the parliamentary Left or the parliamentary Right – both poles shaped by the growth paradigm – we are guaranteed to lose.

We must, therefore, reinvent democracy for our moment in history. We must explore the democratic 'wild' beyond the ballot box, and beyond the increasingly obsolete Left-Right distinction, in order to make political contributions to governance or self-governance in some more coherent and significant way.[2]

So what are our options? What resources do we have to draw on when trying to orientate ourselves in radical political space today?

---

2. To call the Left-Right distinction 'increasingly obsolete' is to make the point that traditionally, and for the most part today, both poles of the political spectrum still operate within an ecocidal growth paradigm. At the same time, I would not wish to deny that there is another sense in which the Left must be reinvented not rejected, and this essay can be interpreted as contributing to that task.

3. Marxism: A Sympathetic Critique

Marxism represents the most prominent alternative to the capitalist mode of economy and representative democracy, so it's an obvious place to begin considering what a radical politics might mean, and a useful point of departure for understanding the politics of wild democracy.

Marx famously argued, with some plausibility, that the state under capitalism is merely an instrument or tool of the capitalist class, meaning that politicians (knowingly or unknowingly) would only enact laws and policies that furthered the narrow interests of that class.[3] To think that political representatives would advance the genuine interests of the working class was dismissed by Marx as 'false consciousness'. Capitalism, he argued, could not be reformed. It had to be replaced.

From this perspective, what is needed is a revolutionary movement, driven by the working class, which would overthrow the capitalist state, abolish private property, and establish state socialism (i.e. social control of the means of production). To oversimplify in the extreme, this new political economy would be defined by the Marxian slogan of distributive justice: 'from each according to their ability, to each according to their needs'. Marx believed that he had uncovered the 'laws of history' and that the inherent contradictions of capitalism would inevitably lead to a communist utopia.

And then the 20th century happened. Various socialist revolutions indeed took place, marching under the banner of Marxism (and Leninism), but in their wake the state was essentially captured by gangs of murderers that employed strategies (e.g., the purges, the gulags, etc.) which neither Marx nor

---

3. In those cases where it seems as if 'democratic' capitalism is being reformed to advance the interests of the working class – for example, by introducing elements of a welfare state – Marx argued that this was merely the capitalist class allowing some steam of discontent to dissipate in order to stabilise the status quo. In fact, Marx sometimes objected to attempts to 'reform' capitalism partly because it let off steam – steam which he felt needed to be directed toward revolutionary activity and mobilisation with the aim of shattering (not reforming) capitalism.

any genuine Marxist would have condoned.[4] That is, *actually existing socialism* was far from the practice of Marxist theory. Certainly, there was no post-revolutionary communist utopia, and ultimately, with the fall of the Berlin Wall in 1989, it seemed the great socialist experiment had demonstrably failed. Capitalism proudly (but no doubt prematurely) declared itself the supreme mode of societal organisation.

What, then, are we to make of Marxism today? Is it still relevant? Don't the representative democracies of free market capitalism represent the proper 'end of history'? Or at least the best we can hope for? These questions require some unpacking.

First, there is a somewhat abstract philosophical point to make. Marx, as noted, claimed that he had uncovered the laws of history – the one and only true way to understand the unfolding of political economy throughout time. Such theoretical confidence may have seemed plausible, even expected, so soon after the Age of Enlightenment, but for us post-Nietzscheans, philosophical times have changed. Today it is said that we live in a postmodern or post-Enlightenment age, defined by 'incredulity toward metanarratives' (Lyotard, 1979: xxiv). This implies a deep scepticism towards 'absolutist' or 'foundationalist' theories of truth or politics, a scepticism informed by philosophical movements such as post-structuralism, neo-pragmatism, and deconstruction.

Without getting into the complexities, these anti-foundationalist philosophical perspectives expose how the world can accommodate various, mutually enriching but not always commensurable interpretations, descriptions, or narratives, each of which conceal as they reveal. In that light, the theoretical dogmatism or 'grand narrative' of Marx needs to be dropped if his theories are to be read with critical eyes, but this can be achieved without most of his ideas losing their force. A political, economic, or social theory does not need to be the one and only

---

4. I will not herein explore the debate about the role of violence in the Marxian revolutionary strategy. While Marx did presume that a violent revolution almost certainly would be necessary, on the grounds that the capitalist class would not voluntarily give up its power, that position can be distinguished from an endorsement from Stalinism. For now, however, I will assume rather than defend that distinction.

truth to shed light on the human condition.

So, if we drop the theoretical overstatements, what insight can Marx offer those of us today who are in search of a coherent, radical politics? His critique of capitalism, to begin with, arguably remains as relevant as ever, even if it needs updating for the 21st century (see, e.g., Hardt and Negri, 2000). Marx fiercely objected to the concentrations of wealth and power produced within capitalist economies and argued that this was not a conditional but an inherent feature of them. Recent evidence seems to support this (Piketty, 2014). Indeed, under globalised capitalism today, the richest eight people now own more than the poorest half of humanity (Hardoon, 2017). No fancy theorising by liberal 'free marketeers' can possibly justify this indigestible disparity of wealth. It *demands* a political response, driven by an outraged citizenry.

Furthermore, as implied above, a strong (though not absolutist) case can be made that the 'superstructure' of democracy and culture under capitalism is insidiously shaped by the 'economic base' of privatised, corporate interests, in ways that entrench the underlying policy aim of profit-maximisation in undemocratic ways. For these reasons, among others, Marx was right to reject capitalism as unjust and undemocratic, and the position of wild democracy expounded and defended in later sections rests, in part, upon this Marxian critique of capitalism.

But what of Marx's revolutionary strategy? And his communist alternative?

To begin with his revolutionary strategy, the reality of the 20th century – culminating in Stalin – must give everyone cause for doubt. Partly as a result of Marx's overblown philosophical rhetoric about having discovered the necessary laws of history, the revolutionary proletarians (especially the leaders) proceeded with religious conviction. They believed they had possession of the Truth and, no matter the cost or compromise, set out to impose it upon the world in the belief (experienced as knowledge) that they were serving the higher cause of justice.

There can be no doubt that 'absolutist' or 'foundationalist' political movements are phenomena of the deepest concern, for the simple but terrifying reason that no 'means' are prohibited if they are rationalised as achieving the desired 'end'. Fundamentalist terrorism, though difficult to define, takes this rationalisation to the logical extreme. Whether political acts are done in the name of God, the Revolution, Free Markets, or the Flying Spaghetti Monster, the very idea of a 'vanguard party' violently taking control of the state and imposing their One True Vision of Utopia on the rest of the world is inherently subject to abuse. 20th-century socialism attests to that with harrowing results.

This is not to say, of course, that Marxist revolutionary strategy *inevitably* leads to Stalinism, only that it *risks* Stalinism, and I would say most people today, including me, consider this a risk too great to take. If state socialism is to be established – an open question for now – the more defensible strategy for transformative change is first to create a politicised culture that desires and demands socialism, and then introduce it via parliamentary democracy. We will critically evaluate this strategy of 'democratic socialism' below, as it informs wild democracy while being distinct from it.

In any case, as noted above, the post-structuralist critique of Truth with a capital T has kicked the epistemological foundations out from beneath any One True Vision of Utopia and thus also from beneath the epistemological foundations of the traditional Marxist revolutionary strategy. Capitalism may be unjust, but there is not one, single conception of a just alternative that should be imposed upon society by an enlightened, revolutionary vanguard party. Again, there may be one 'no' but there are and should be many 'yeses', both in terms of a just, sustainable and flourishing 'ideal society' and in terms the best strategy for moving toward it. Everything, always, is context-dependent, which calls for theoretical humility and warns against universalist political statements or strategies. For even if a global moral or political code emerged, this would still require interpretation and application in context-specific ways.[5]

---

5. To reject universalism, of course, does not imply a crude relativism or conservativism accepting that any politics is as good as any other. This is not the place, however, to explore that thorny issue.

With respect to Marx's vision of a communist alternative, he did not provide much detail, other than the obvious fact that private property would be abolished and the means of production would come under social control. For present purposes, the critical point to make is that his vision was embedded, regrettably, in the 'productivist' growth paradigm almost as much as capitalism was and is. We can hardly blame Marx for this blind spot, however, because he was writing at a time when the environmental effects of industrialisation were only just beginning to show themselves. That is, he wrote in an age before climate change, peak oil concerns, topsoil erosion, biodiversity loss, etc. were factors that any coherent politics had to address. The earth was not yet 'full'. The Anthropocene had not yet set in.

Nevertheless, knowing what we know now, Marxism (and socialism more broadly) must undergo a deep revision in order to remain relevant in our era of overlapping environmental crises (see, e.g., Foster, 2000). First and foremost this means transcending the ecocidal economics of growth. Promisingly, this theoretical revision is well underway, with a sophisticated body of scholarship on eco-socialism developing in recent years (see, e.g., Sarkar, 1999; Foster, 2000; Baer, 2016).

The essential logic of eco-socialism can be easily summarised: if capitalism has a 'growth imperative' built into its structure, and limitless growth is environmentally unsupportable, then capitalism is incompatible with sustainability (see Smith, 2016). Therefore, if sustainability is to be taken seriously – and we are all environmentalists now, aren't we? – capitalism must be replaced with a post-growth or steady-state form of eco-socialism that operates within planetary limits. In the most developed regions of the world, this environmental equilibrium must be preceded by a phase of planned economic contraction, or 'degrowth'. Obviously, degrowth by definition is incompatible with the growth imperative of capitalism, so here we have an environmental logic to support the social justice logic forcefully presented by Marx: capitalism cannot be reformed; it has to be replaced. This line of reasoning informs wild democracy and will be examined more closely below.

Although far from being a homogenous body of work, the emerging body of eco-socialist and degrowth scholarship provides some of the most coherent political platforms on offer today, although, admittedly, both the movements remain marginalised and almost insignificant political forces, despite their coherency and potential. It also remains an open question whether eco-socialism and degrowth should attempt to be established democratically 'from above' via the apparatus of the state, or driven into existence democratically 'from below' via grassroots movements. This question provides a smooth segue into a consideration of the politics of anarchism, which will provide further resources to draw upon when the time comes to sketch an outline of wild democracy.

4. Anarchism: A Sympathetic Critique

Anarchism is a political worldview and practice that rejects, not rules, but rulers. Despite being a diverse school, it is defined, if through nothing else, by its rejection of the state, of all governmental claims to authority. To speak generally, anarchists believe that governments are inherently illegitimate concentrations of political power and that the ideal form of societal organisation is stateless, without centralised or 'representative' government. Many or most anarchists choose not to vote in elections out of principle, not wanting to be complicit in, or confer a sense of legitimacy on, a representative mode of government they reject.

But far from advocating 'chaos' – as mainstream media too often portray the anarchist agenda – the meaning of anarchy can be understood as *order, security, justice, and freedom through cooperative self-governance*. Anarchists believe that human beings do not need to be governed, as such. Instead, anarchists believe that we are capable of working together to govern ourselves, by way of local, participatory political engagement. In its broadest terms, this is the basic anarchist vision of an ideal society, and it implies that the best strategy for moving toward such a society is for individuals and communities to live the new world into existence, here and now, without employing state support (and probably receiving a lot of state resistance).

Given that anarchists do not recognise the legitimacy of the state, they are often prepared to engage in acts of civil disobedience if the laws in question strike their considered moral conscience as being unjust. In the words typically attributed to Thomas Jefferson: 'When injustice becomes law, rebellion becomes duty.' There is a long and honourable tradition embracing this right to civil disobedience, inspired by revered figures such as Henry Thoreau, Mahatma Gandhi, Emma Goldman, and Martin Luther King, Jnr (not all of whom identify as anarchists, of course).

This is not the forum to present a detailed definition, history, critique, or defence of anarchism. The primary purpose of addressing anarchism presently is to highlight its theoretical and practical antagonism with Marxism and, through that analysis, highlight the core issues relevant to wild democracy.

The defining antagonism between anarchism and Marxism lies, obviously, in the differing roles the state is assumed to play in the transition to a post-capitalist society. Whereas Marxism sees the state as being *central* and *necessary* to that transition, anarchists – at least, anarchists of classical disposition – believe the state both should not and could not be the tool through which the ideal society is established. Other strains of anarchism argue that, if necessary, the state should be captured by anarchists via the democratic process (or, if necessary, through revolution) in order to initiate the process of decentralising the state out of existence. That is, capture the state for the purpose of abolishing the state.

It is worth noting that, even under Marxism, the communist utopia is assumed, eventually, to be without need of a state. In the words of Engels (1969), eventually the state under advanced communism will 'wither way' and be replaced merely with an 'administration of things'. This is important, because it shows that there is no necessary clash between Marxists and anarchists in their conception of the ideal society – both are stateless. The defining antagonism is with respect to the state's role in the transition.

Given that the question of 'transition' is central to understanding political engagement today, this is not a tangential or inconsequential debate within radical politics. Rejecting the need for the state, anarchists practice what is sometimes called 'prefigurative politics'. This involves engaging in direct action, in order to 'build the new world within the shell of the old', as the anarchist slogan goes – infusing daily life and interactions with the ethics of mutual respect, freedom, and non-coercion.

There is something very attractive, even compelling, about the immediacy, directness, and lived commitment of anarchism. To employ the famous Gandhian dictum for anarchist purposes: 'be the change you wish to see in the world'. The idea is that if enough people adopt and apply this attitude, the world will change, without the need for taking state power. Do not make demands of the state – it will ignore you. Do not wait for the Revolution – it may never arrive (or if it does, it will fail to live up to its ideals). Just get active in your local community and start building the new world today. And if it turns out you are alone building the new world, or the social movement is too small to achieve its ambitions, then at least you are living out your values with integrity and authenticity.

One of the most common objections to anarchism is framed in terms of 'human nature'. The criticism is that anarchism sounds nice in theory, perhaps, but it would not work in practice, over the long term, at least, because generally human beings are too weak, selfish, or lazy to be able to function without a government that structures the world with laws, deterrents, and incentives. Of course, there have been successful 'anarchist moments' in history (e.g., the Spanish experiments) that provide some support for anarchism functioning well in practice, but the fact that these anarchist societies have tended to be short-lived also means the case is inconclusive. Indigenous societies arguably provide more interesting examples of the long-term functionality of societies without a state, but obviously the application of those modes of existence to the 21st-century world is no straightforward matter.

Many anarchists indeed have a very positive view of human nature, embracing some conception of 'basic goodness'. They argue that the apparent flaws in human nature are actually just a result of capitalism spoiling our basic goodness, by incentivising competition, celebrating greed, and creating social anxieties and insecurities through manipulative marketing strategies. When an anarchist society is established, it is argued, people will see that human beings are inherently capable of living co-operatively without state coercion. Indeed, there is evidence from evolutionary biology indicating that those species (or societies) based on cooperation rather than competition are most likely to prevail in the long term.

In any case, anarchists can turn the human nature objection on its head, arguing that if human beings *are* inherently weak and greedy, that is all the more reason not to create a centralised and powerful state, because flawed humans inevitably must run that state! Better to minimise the concentrations of power.

I think, however, there is a more sophisticated response to the human nature objection, and that is to deny that there is such a thing as a fixed 'human nature' that we are born with. Granted, human beings are products of a long evolutionary history that doubtless shapes our psychological constitution, but ultimately we are free, as the existentialists argued, to *choose our nature* through our decisions (which means we have no pre-determined nature, as such – humans are neither inherently good nor inherently bad). Our 'existence precedes our essence'.

From this perspective, it is a manoeuvre of 'bad faith' to talk of a pre-determined nature because that just deflects attention away from our inescapable responsibility to shape ourselves. Nevertheless, insofar as we are 'socially constructed' beings, shaped by our cultural and institutional contexts – which cannot be denied – it still remains open for us to 'reconstruct' ourselves and our contexts according to our own visions of what humanity could become. As Jean-Paul Sartre (1965: 9:101) once said: 'you can always make something out of what you've been made into.'[6]

Like classical socialism, classical anarchism needs to be revised in light of the environmental predicament. Traditionally, anarchists saw the state as the primary enemy. Today, however, that focus seems too narrow. After all, we could conceive of an anarcho-capitalist society that had abolished the state but nevertheless remained shaped by an economics of growth, leaving the question of sustainability (and therefore justice) unresolved. Anarchism, therefore, must evolve into eco-anarchism to remain relevant, and this revision has been led by figures such as Murray Bookchin and Ted Trainer.[7] Whereas democratic eco-socialists, as we have seen, tend to argue that a post-growth or steady-state economy should be designed and instituted via the apparatus of the state, eco-anarchists often envision a similar 'ideal society' but argue that it should be (or can only be) produced through localised grassroots activity, where individuals and communities essentially create the new society themselves, without state support.

While the anarchist imperative to 'build the new world within the shell of the old' has much to recommend it, there are many deep and powerful structures and vested interests that obstruct that strategy. Eco-anarchists believe those obstacles can be overcome without need of the state. Eco-socialists argue that transforming those structures requires state action. This is the key debate that will now be examined more closely.

---

6. The 'social construction' of human nature, however, does give rise to a 'chicken and egg' problem for anarchists. In short, an anarchist society would create the social conditions conducive to positive and cooperative human relations, but we must begin from where we are, within a capitalist society that socially constructs human nature in selfish ways that may make anarchist modes of social organisation unworkable or at least more challenging. Put otherwise, which comes first: the anarchist society that shapes a cooperative human nature? Or the cooperative human nature that creates the functioning anarchist society? Socialists face the same problem.

7. In this chapter I am defining eco-socialism in terms of state-instituted eco-socialism. It is important to acknowledge, however, that most anarchists are 'socialists' too, in the sense that they believe the most important means of production should be under 'social control' (primarily if not exclusively) rather than be held as private property. So the distinction between eco-socialist and eco-anarchism in this chapter is primarily for the purpose of highlighting differing views on the role the state should play in the transition beyond capitalism.

5. Beyond (and between) Anarchism and Marxism

Let me focus this critical analysis by reiterating the strengths of democratic eco-socialism. There is much with which to sympathise in this emerging political theory. First, it recognises, unlike reformist political movements, that capitalism cannot be reformed but has to be replaced; secondly, it recognises that any coherent socialism today must transcend growth economics; and, thirdly, it avoids the dangers inherent in revolutionary Marxism (or Leninism) by rejecting the need for a 'vanguard party' to capture the state through violence, instead calling for the democratically mandated institution of eco-socialism via the mechanisms of parliament.

Moreover, democratic eco-socialism recognises the reality that structures and systems within which we live deeply shape and influence the forms of living that are available to us. It is all well and good for anarchists to try to ignore the state to death, or ignore capitalism to death, but from the perspective of democratic eco-socialism, that may be naïve. Any anarchist movement may well find itself structurally locked into ways of living that do not accord with anarchist values, leaving activists with little time, energy, or capacity to engage in acts of resistance and renewal. Change the structures, however, in line with an eco-socialist agenda, and new ways of living and being may emerge or be possible. New eco-socialist structures may even *permit* anarchism to flourish.

The urgency with which change needs to occur is another strength of the eco-socialist position. Even if it would be more desirable for grassroots movements to progressively 'build the new world within the shell of the old', a case can be made that the depth and urgency of the transition needed requires centralised state action. Establishing things like new public transport networks or bike lanes, or new energy systems, or new banking, monetary, or property systems, while conceivably achieved in a developed anarchist society, are arguably more readily achievable in the short term via state policy.

Similarly, in a crisis or collapse situation – far from being
an unrealistic scenario – it could also be the case that the
state is needed simply to maintain and administer the most
basic social services and infrastructure (e.g., electricity, water,
hospitals, food rationing, etc). What Brendan Gleeson (2015)
calls a 'Guardian State' may be required in such times to avoid
complete societal breakdown and the suffering that economic
or ecosystemic collapse would bring. Such a crisis could also be
a (tragic) opportunity to re-draw the contours of the economy,
informed by eco-socialist values. Obviously, it would be better
to plan and design such an economy *in advance* of collapse,
but in cynical moods one can easily think that the conditions of
instability needed for genuine change will not come about until
the crises of capitalism deepen and intensify further. Of course,
what is produced in the wake of such deep instability can take
any number of forms – the challenge being to make the best of
it, and above all to protect democracy.

There are also global structures – such as international trade
agreements – which could be influenced more coherently via
an eco-socialist government than via the strategies of eco-anarchism. For example, the Transpacific Partnership agreement
threatens to impoverish democracy and further entrench the
neoliberal agenda. If this comes into force, it will be that much
harder for eco-anarchists (and eco-socialists) to advance their
cause. There are many such examples that could be provided,
suggesting that anarchists ignore the state at their own peril.

Traditional anarchists, of course, would reject this state-
driven transition strategy, first, because it requires working with
and through the (allegedly illegitimate) mechanisms of the state;
and second, eco-anarchists tend to argue that a centralised state
simply cannot adequately manage the diversity of local contexts
sufficiently well to meet and address local needs. From this perspective, only self-governing local communities can know the
particular needs and features of their community, so centralised
planning must be rejected as being too blunt an instrument to
be effective or efficient. In fact, the defence of eco-socialism
above could even be inverted in defence of eco-anarchism, that

is to say, in a context of crisis or collapse, we may not be able to rely on state administration of the situation, and thus we must learn the art of self-governance today.

Furthermore, eco-anarchists question the very possibility of a post-capitalist transition driven by the state. We live in a globalised capitalist economy, in which it has never been easier for capital, with the tap of a few computer keys, to move from nation to nation. This means the moment any government seems to be mobilising for an eco-socialist agenda, this will most likely induce 'capital flight' and/or provoke economic turmoil or collapse by scaring the stock market. There is also the geopolitical problem, as being the first to initiate an eco-socialist degrowth transition would likely imply a state having less funds available for military forces, weakening a nation's relative power globally. Can we imagine a state voluntarily weakening its geopolitical position of power?

One eco-socialist response would be that the transition must be *global*, but this gives rise to the problem of being the 'first mover'. For example, it may be that globalised eco-socialism could avoid capital flight – there would be nowhere to fly to! – but this would require a near-simultaneous global transition, which, for the foreseeable future, seems breathtakingly implausible.[8]

A related anarchist criticism of democratic eco-socialism is that by the time any mass movement for eco-socialism had emerged, the post-capitalist transition would have or should have already been completed, or mostly completed. That is, by the time there is a broad culture that wants eco-socialism, the social movement would have already created the new society via grassroots participatory action. This strategy also provides one way to deal with the critical issue noted in the previous paragraph. Rather than risk capital flight or economic collapse,

---

8. Granted, a large-scale eco-anarchist social movement seems equally implausible at present, but eco-anarchism has the advantage of getting immediately to work trying to establish new, localised, and more self-sufficient and collaborative modes of economy, rather than making demands of the state. Even if this eco-anarchist strategy fails to produce a sustainable society, it may at least help increase resilience.

or wait for a globalised eco-socialist movement to take root, the anarchist strategy would involve building the New Economy B under and within Old Economy A, in such a way that could avoid the destabilising effects of a 'top down' implementation of eco-socialism (see Trainer, 2010).

Even from this cursory critical review, it is clear that there are tensions – perhaps irresolvable tensions – between eco-socialists and eco-anarchists. Does that mean we have to choose one or the other? Do the points in conflict require these two forms of radical politics to oppose each other? Or, despite the points of conflict, can we reorientate ourselves in political space in such a way that somehow acknowledges and at the same time accommodates these theoretical and practical tensions?

It is the purpose of wild democracy to carve out such a space, and with the background theoretical groundwork complete, a preliminary statement of wild democracy can at last be made, which weaves together the threads of the preceding analysis.

6. Wild Democracy: A Biodiversity of Resistance and Renewal

In a politico-cultural context gripped by growth fetishism, it would be a dereliction of duty to think that voting in elections consummates one's political or civic duty. It would be different, perhaps, if our representatives were acting with wisdom, integrity, and foresight – clearly serving the causes of justice and sustainability – but they are in fact doing the opposite, despite what wonderful-sounding things they might say. Thus, we find ourselves within a regressive representative democracy, which is where we must begin. So be it. How then is one to contribute to a radical democratic politics today?

Let us acknowledge, first, that voting itself is not much of a burden. It typically takes less than an hour, once every three or four years, so I propose that even radicals who have lost faith in representative democracy should still vote as strategically as possible (which is always a context dependent issue) and to take that act as the 'starting gun' of political participation, not the finish line. I should think that most democratic eco-socialists would agree with this.

Hard-nosed anarchists may object that voting implicates one in an illegitimate form of government and is therefore an inappropriate means of political change, but less dogmatic and more pragmatic anarchists may accept that voting for the 'least evil' of competing political parties could help provide a modestly better starting place to advance anarchism and therefore voting should be considered *one tool* in the anarchist tool belt (even if it is an almost insignificant tool).

Furthermore, a pragmatic anarchist may defend voting on the grounds that in a more enlightened socio-cultural context, there is scope for an anarchist politics to actually push state governments toward a policy of decentralisation, which would be a step in the right direction, potentially culminating in the state 'withering way' in line with the shared desires and visions of anarchists and Marxists. Indeed, the idea of (one day) taking control of the state in order to dissolve the state is a coherent political position (see Fotopoulos, 1997), one that I feel pragmatic eco-anarchists should share with eco-socialists. And even if the stateless utopia is never achieved, I would argue that transcending the dystopia of centralised state capitalism is still a worthy goal.

Whatever the case, the first premise of wild democracy is simply that *voting does not end one's civic duty*, which itself is a radical statement in today's largely apolitical cultures. For the foreseeable future, at least, and possibly forever, a citizen's most important political contributions can only take place 'in the wild', beyond the mechanisms of representative democracy.

Now, having voted (or having conscientiously objected to voting), one is again faced with the question: how should one contribute now to a radical politics in the most strategically effective way? This seems to present a fork in the road, whereby eco-anarchists and eco-socialists must part company: eco-anarchists should set out to live the new world into existence, while eco-socialists should establish a political party or attempt to influence existing political parties to push an eco-socialist agenda through parliament.

Each side of this divide currently accuses the other of pursuing the wrong strategy, and the in-fighting begins. In an attempt to stem that infighting, which I consider a waste of oppositional energy, I want to suggest that if this fork in the road exists, *we are not yet at such a fork*. That is, here and now, there is so much work to be done raising cultural consciousness about the need to transcend capitalism and move beyond the ecocidal economics of growth that eco-anarchists and eco-socialists can and should proceed more often as allies, at least for the foreseeable future. Certainly, it is too early to try to get eco-socialist ideas through parliament because there is not yet anywhere near a mandate for such ideas. That would be to put the cart before the horse.[9] After all, the recent Australian election was campaigned primarily on the issue of which party could grow the economy best. Obviously, the culture-shift must get well underway in advance of any culturally digestible political campaign for eco-socialism.

In fact, such a culture-shift may even begin (and only begin) in the soil of subjectivity – in a 'politics of the subject' – implying that we are being called to resist or refuse the apolitical, consumerist subjectivities which capitalist culture has tired to impose on us – and to create someone new. That is, we must rewild our subjectivities in order to be better citizens of and for an ecozoic era.

Therefore, I contend that the primary task today, both for eco-anarchists and eco-socialists, is to provoke a cultural revolution in consciousness. First and foremost, this can take the form of consciousness-raising and education activities and strategies, but in line with traditional anarchist strategies, it should also take the form of resistance and renewal. That is, resisting the most egregious aspects of the status quo (protesting, direct action, civil disobedience, etc.) as well as engaging in acts of 'prefigurative politics' that create or demonstrate

---

9. Some eco-socialists accept this and argue that attempts to win political power should be deferred 'until pressure for change in the direction of eco-socialism ha[s] built up in several countries'. Saral Sarkar (1999) p: 230.

small-scale examples of new post-capitalist modes of existence. Not only do those small-scale demonstrations function to begin the dauntingly large task of 'building the new world within the shell of the old', they can also be justified on the grounds of being a practical form of education. After all, being exposed to new experiments in living can be one of the most effective ways to engage people about the issues motivating the experiments. Nothing persuades, inspires, or educates quite like a real world example of a new mode of living and being, even on a small-scale. And eco-socialists and eco-anarchists are likely to share a great deal in terms of what a prefigurative politics should look like (e.g., non-consumerist, egalitarian, community-orientated sustainable experiments that challenge capitalist economic relations as far as possible).

From the anarchist perspective, these three (infinitely diverse, context-dependent) practices of education, resistance, and renewal, are the most defensible strategies to adopt. But I would argue also that *at this early stage* of the post-capitalism transition, it makes sense for eco-socialists to adopt, support, and encourage these same strategies, in the hope of building a social movement that, in time, could provide the mandate for an eco-socialist agenda in parliament. Indeed, I think that anarchists should not be bothered by eco-socialists advocating their bold legislative agendas because (even if one rejects centralised government) the visions of eco-socialism can help people see that 'other worlds are possible'.

This opening or rewilding of the imagination is not an insignificant precondition of transformative change. There will be no deliberate transition beyond capitalism – whether eco-socialist, eco-anarchist, or another other way – until more people see that other worlds are possible. In that light, all visions of alternative modes of living should be encouraged in order to help ignite people's revolutionary imaginations. We need a flourishing biodiversity of resistance and renewal.[10] The real problem today isn't so much getting the alternative vision or visions *correct*

---

10. I borrow the phrase 'biodiversity of resistance' from Arundhati Roy.

(although, of course, that should always be the aim). The real problem, I contend, is figuring out how to open up people's imaginations to the *very possibility* of alternative modes of existence. Too often today we hear that it is easier to imagine the end of the world than the end of capitalism. All radical imaginations must unite to overcome or deconstruct this tragic, powerful, but invisible obstacle – or all else is lost.

Furthermore, we need to think carefully about how a successful transition might transpire. Eco-anarchists might well argue, as noted above, that we will never need a state-driven eco-socialism, because by the time there is enough social support for an eco-socialist agenda to be passed through parliament, the grassroots social movement should already have been able to create the new world. That is a perspective worth taking seriously, however it risks jumping from a completely capitalist culture to a completely eco-anarchist culture too sharply. The transition, after all, is likely to take some time, and as the eco-anarchist movement grows, it is quite possible that the emerging social movement – midway through, for example – could influence parliamentary politics (and certainly local politics) in ways that actually advance the eco-anarchist cause. I maintain that it would be better to achieve anarchism with the partial and temporary support of the state than not achieve anarchism at all.

For all these reasons, I am again inclined to suggest that the ongoing conflict between eco-anarchists and eco-socialists may be, to a large extent, misconceived. In other words, it seems to me that if an eco-anarchist movement were to emerge strongly in culture, it may find it expedient, at some stage, to use the state to advance the eco-anarchist agenda, and at that point eco-anarchists may well be grateful that there is a developed tradition of democratic eco-socialism that has thought deeply about the best 'policies' for eco-socialism. Indeed, if this approach were successful, we can imagine the policies for eco-socialism first decentralising the state and then allowing, even encouraging, the state to 'wither away'.

In this light eco-anarchism and eco-socialism can be conceived of as being two sides of the same coin of wild democracy.

On the eco-anarchist side, the political task is to get active building the new world, raising consciousness about the necessity of degrowth, and resisting the most egregious aspects of the status quo, in order to build a new, engaged, post-capitalist consciousness. On the eco-socialist side of the coin, the task is to assist and support in the building of this grassroots post-capitalist movement through similar acts of education, resistance, and renewal, while at the same time developing a legislative agenda that, when the social movement is strong enough, could coherently restructure society in ways that would more easily *permit* and *encourage* local, highly self-reliant, eco-communities to govern themselves – beyond a centralised state.

7. Conclusion

The purpose of this chapter was to try to carve out a space for cooperation between radical, post-capitalist schools of political thought and practice that both historically and today tend to conceive of themselves as opposed. There are certainly some factions which will be dissatisfied: first, those who advocate violent revolution as the only coherent strategy to bring an end to capitalism; second, 'reformists' who think that capitalism can be regulated to advance the causes of justice and sustainability; and thirdly, those strict anarchists who reject any political strategy that entails working through the mechanisms of parliament (even if engagement with the state is for the sole purpose of advancing anarchist causes).

Another potential point of contention more broadly might be a claim that wild democracy, as outlined, can actually be accommodated within eco-anarchism and/or eco-socialism as they exist. To that objection I say: good! We are on the same page. The analysis, even so, would not have been redundant. By unpacking the tensions and antagonisms between these two necessary schools of radical politics, and highlighting the different challenges facing each perspective, it is hoped that the relationship between them is better understood and the potential for collaborative activism clearer.

One point on my mind throughout has been the troubling fact that mainstream culture today tends to be instinctively put off by both the terms 'anarchism' and 'socialism' – let alone 'degrowth'! This is doubtless owing to a conscious effort by the powers-that-be to undermine any sense of there being an alternative to capitalism. This should prompt us to think seriously about how best to share our ideas and perspectives with others. Wouldn't it be foolish, for example, to ignore the fact that the term 'anarchism' has been so misleadingly presented in mainstream culture that using it could often do more harm than good, at least to some audiences? The same goes for eco-socialism and degrowth, two terms that also have huge public relations challenges. If a mass movement is what is needed and desired by these various radical imaginations, then recognising the importance of 'marketing' or 'presenting' our visions in the best way possible is an issue that cannot be dismissed as unimportant or tangential.

It may seem theoretically unnecessary, even lacking in intellectual integrity, to think about how best to 'brand' one's political perspectives. Shouldn't we just be as clear as possible, even if culture isn't ready for us? Despite being theoretically sound, that perspective is pragmatically or politically naïve. We can't just be 'right'. We also need to be 'heard', and that means being cognisant of the diversity of audiences and the differing vocabularies that may need to be used to maximise our engagement with differing audiences. Admittedly, this is not theoretically or conceptually neat – there is a tendency to desire a single banner under which the Great Transition should march, in the hope of unifying diverse threads of opposition. But the position of wild democracy holds that our broad post-capitalist cause may be best served by using a multitude of vocabularies. Indeed, this is part of why wild democracy is 'wild'. It defies and resists singular expression.

In fact, we see this diversity of expressions already in existence today. Just think of the range of activities and movements that could easily be considered elements of wild democracy:

transition towns; the divestment movement; sharing networks; intentional communities and ecovillages; permaculture groups; Occupy; manifestations of the gift economy; the voluntary simplicity and tiny house movements; deliberative democracy; community energy projects; activist hubs; artist hubs; alternative journalism websites; volunteer groups; farmers' markets; re-skilling workshops; charities; progressive non-profit enterprises and worker cooperatives; and the ever-expanding network of radical environmental and social justice groups that exist across the cultural landscape. The list could go on.

Although beyond conventional political classification, wild democracy, in these various forms, can be seen already growing out of the ever-widening cracks of a globalised capitalism in decline, as yet unaware of its potential to re-enchant the political spirit of our times.

None of these movements or approaches have all the answers but arguably all of them will need to play a role moving beyond the dystopia of capitalism. Of course, they risk being easily accommodated and subsumed by the existing order of things. The important point is for each of these movements for change to continually reflect on the question of 'strategy'; the question of how best can we direct our limited energies, time, and resources to advance the necessary causes of justice and sustainability. That question, however, does not allow for a generalisable answer. Political engagement is always relative to our contexts; relative to our unique set of skills, limitations, connections, and responsibilities. We are left with no firmer ground to stand upon than the potential of our imaginations to creatively engage the present as we move forward together into an uncertain future. But that is ground enough to proceed without despair. Our greatest fear should be that our modes of resistance become conservative rather than transgressive.

There is obviously much more to be said on all these issues. Let me close by simply acknowledging that now, when asked whether I am an eco-anarchist or an eco-Marxist, I can say I am at once *both* and *neither*. Or, less paradoxically but more boldly, *we* radicals can say, in the spirit of solidarity, that we inhabit that heterogeneous space beyond 'normal' politics – sojourning passionately and compassionately in the democratic wild – where futures are unfolding experimentally in the present flow of revolt.

In the words of Henry Thoreau (1983): 'This world is but a canvas to the imagination.'

References

Baer, H. 2016. *Toward a democratic eco-socialism as the next world system*, report to The Next World System Project, 28 April, 2016.

Bookchin, M. 1990. *Remaking society: Pathways to a green future*, South End Press, Boston.

Derrida, J. 2010. *Spectres of Marx: The state of the debt, the work of mourning and the new international*, Routledge, London.

Dewey, J. 1981–90. *The later works: Volume 13*, ed. Jo Ann Boydston, Southern Illinois University Press, Carbondale.

Engels, F. 1969. *Anti-Duhring*, Progress Publishers, Moscow.

Foster, J.B. 2000. *Marx's ecology: Materialism and nature*, Monthly Review Press, New York.

Fotopoulos, T. 1997. *Towards an inclusive democracy: The crisis of the growth economy and the need for a new liberatory project*, Cassell, London.

Gleeson, B. 2015. *The urban condition*, Routledge, London.

Hardoon, D. 2017. 'An economy for the 99%', Oxfam Briefing Paper, Summary, January 2017.

Hardt, M. and Negri, A. 2000. *Empire*, Harvard University Press, Boston.

Lyotard, J.-F. 1979. *The postmodern condition: A report on knowledge*, University of Minnesota Press, Minnesota.

Meadows, D., Randers, J., and Meadows, D. 2004. *Limits to growth: The 30-year update*, Chelsea Green Publishing, White River Junction.

Newman, S. 2010. *The politics of postanarchism*, Edinburgh University Press, Edinburgh.

Piketty, T. 2014. *Capital in the twenty-first century*, Harvard University Press, Boston.

Sarkar, S. 1999. *Eco-socialism or eco-capitalism: A critical analysis of humanity's fundamental choices*, Zed Books, London.

Sartre, J.-P. 1965. *Situations*, George Braziller, New York.

Smith, R. 2016. *Green capitalism: The god that failed*, College Publications, London.

Thoreau, H. 1983. *The portable Thoreau*, ed. Carl Bode, Penguin, London.

Trainer, T. 2010. *The transition to a sustainable and just world*, Enviro-book, Sydney.

8

A PROSPEROUS DESCENT: TELLING NEW STORIES AS THE OLD BOOK CLOSES

Nothing is harder, yet nothing is more necessary, than to speak of certain things whose existence is neither demonstrable nor probable. The very fact that serious and conscientious people treat them as existing things brings them a step closer to existence and to the possibility of being born.
– Herman Hesse

Over the last two centuries in the West, we have been telling ourselves that economic growth is the most direct path to prosperity, that the good life implies material affluence, and that technology and 'free markets' will be able to solve most of our social and environmental problems. In recent decades, we have even attempted to impose this story on the entire globe, arrogantly declaring the end of history.

As each day passes, however, this story becomes less credible, its future less plausible. With disarming clarity we see, and increasingly feel, that the global economy is degrading the ecological foundations of life, threatening a catastrophe that in fact is already well underway. The fact that capitalism also produces abhorrent inequalities of wealth raises the questions: for whom do we destroy the planet? And to what end? We are told to wait for justice, as if in a Kafkaesque novel, but we are not told how long we must wait.

As if this were not enough, the assault of capitalism strikes deeper still, to the core of our being. Consumer culture is spreading a spiritual malaise, an apathetic sadness of the soul, as ever-more people discover that material things cannot satisfy the universal human craving for meaning. Our abundance of stuff, as technology forecaster Paul Saffo argues, has merely produced new scarcities, creating an existential void that stuff simply cannot fill.

As our culture continues to pursue this uninspired, narrowly materialistic conception of the good life, we are guilty of celebrating a gross failure of imagination and mistaken ideas of freedom and wealth.

We know, deep down, that something is very wrong with this cultural narrative – that there must be better, freer, more humane ways to live. But we live in a world that conspires to keep knowledge of such alternatives from us. We are told that consumerism is the peak of civilisation and that there are no alternatives, and over time, as these messages are endlessly repeated and normalised, our imaginations begin to contract and we lose the ability to envision different worlds.

The future was hurtling towards us; then it arrived; now it is behind us. The new future isn't what it used to be. And yet, it seems we have not yet found a new story by which to live. We are the generation between stories, desperately clinging to yesterday's but uncertain of tomorrow's. Adrift in the cosmos, without a narrative in which to lay down new roots, humanity marches on, naively attempting to solve the crises of civilisation with the same kind of thinking that caused them.

But then again, perhaps the new words we need are already with us.

Perhaps we just need to live them into existence.

◆ ◆ ◆

Buckminster Fuller, an American architect and systems theorist, once said: 'You never change things by fighting the existing reality. To change something, build a new model that makes the existing model obsolete.' This approach to social transformation essentially expresses the idea that examples are powerful, that examples can send ripples through culture further than we might think possible, creating cultural currents that can turn into subcultures, that sometimes explode into social movements and that, on very rare occasions, can spark a revolution in consciousness that changes the world. In an age when it can sometimes seem as if there is no alternative to the carbon-intensive, consumer way of life, being exposed to a real-world example of a new way of living and being has the potential to expand and radicalise the ecological imagination. At such times, when we close our eyes, new, more hopeful futures flicker in and out of existence, forcing us to vote for a future where once we had thought there was no alternative to our casual, progressive ecocide.

This experience of possibility can be both exhilarating and terrifying, for in those moments when we are able to break through the crust of conventional thinking we see that the world, as it is, is not how it has to be. Faced with living proof that life can be different – if only, at first, in a microcosm – the structures and narratives that define the contours of the human situation can suddenly seem less compelling. In this way, lived examples of alternative modes of being-on-Earth can challenge us to be examples ourselves – can challenge us to live experimentally within the cracks of capitalism in the hope of setting ourselves free. Nothing mobilises a community of people quite like the taste of freedom. Soon enough, in the flow of revolt, the new model makes the old model obsolete.

This is the disruptive potential of even small-scale explorations of new ways of living and being. When shaping post-capitalist forms of life, however, one has to start somewhere – within capitalism – with nothing but bold intentions and reckless hope. It follows that the efforts of those who seek to break new paths in the cultural landscape and signal new directions must inevitably seem insignificant at first. Pioneers are easily dismissed as utopian dreamers or escapists who lack a sense of political reality. But just as vision without politics is naive, politics without vision is dangerous. We must dream before we shape our politics, or else we will never awaken from the existing nightmare of pragmatism without principle. We are all utopians and always have been; only some of us are more ambitious.

◆ ◆ ◆

Telling new stories about humanity's place on Earth, and trying to live those stories into existence, has been the ongoing challenge a few of us set ourselves over the last two years on a humble but beautiful eight-hectare property in the Gunai district of Gippsland, south-east Victoria. In ways that I will try to explain, the distinction between life and literature has begun to blur, providing fertile soil for a new paradigm, a new politics of possibility, to take root. The fact that Gippsland is one of the most carbon-intensive places on Earth merely provides an ironic backdrop against which our experiments in living differently can be contrasted.

The green shoots of this project first pushed through the soil after one of the owners of the Gippsland property read my book *Entropia: Life Beyond Industrial Civilisation* (2013), which is a work of utopian fiction set after the demise of industrial civilisation on an isolated island in the South Pacific. The book envisions a radically 'simple living' culture and a post-growth economy that emerged after the 'Great Disruption', describing a way of life based on material sufficiency, frugality, renewable energy, local economy, appropriate technology, and self-governance.

On the final page, I invited any interested readers to be in touch if they wanted to try to establish a real-world demonstration project that somehow embodied the ideas, vision, and utopian ambitions of the book.

To my utter surprise, but much to my delight, within a few weeks of publication I received an email from an inspired fellow called Mortimer Flynn wanting to take up the challenge, noting that he was a 'steward' of some land – not an owner, he insisted, but someone who held land 'in trust' for future generations.

There were also some limited funds available to get things started. He invited me out to view the property and the rest, as they say, is history. The preface of a new story had been written.

On the day I first visited, sitting on the edge of the dam in the filtered shade of softly swaying gum trees, Mortimer and I shared ideas and viewpoints on why we thought demonstrating a simpler, more localised, less consumptive way of life was a worthwhile endeavour; why we thought it was necessary to try to build the new world within the shell of the old, no matter our chances of success. To cut a long story short, our 'theory of change' was simply that examples can be powerful.

Our united motivation arose from a deep frustration and disappointment with mainstream politics, combined with a complete lack of faith that things would change from the top. We saw the world ablaze with overlapping crises – cultural, economic, environmental – and yet our politicians were bickering over this, tinkering with that, all the while the ship of civilisation propelled itself ever closer to the rocks.

It seemed to us that if a new world was to emerge, it would have to be driven into existence 'from below' – by ordinary people like us doing it ourselves. We were under no illusions about the significance of our efforts, of course, despite our lofty ambitions. Every life is but a drop in the ocean.

But that just makes it all the more important that our humble contributions are made to count.

As well as sharing a profound discontent with the many short-sighted failings of parliamentary democracy, Mortimer and I shared a mutual concern over mainstream environmentalism. Everywhere, environmentalists were calling on people to recycle, use efficient light bulbs, take shorter showers, and compost – which are all good and sensible things, of course. But focusing on small-scale household action gives the impression that we can consume our way to a green economy without having to significantly change the way we live. It gives the impression that there is no need to change consumerist social values or the fundamentals of a growth-orientated market economy, for the dominant ideology suggests that technology, eco-design, and free markets will save us from ourselves; apparently, more growth can solve the problems growth is causing. We didn't buy that.

As 'green consumerism' and 'green growth' were being celebrated by media, businesses, and politicians, and seemingly swallowed whole by the great majority, we saw environmental science becoming ever more depressing, raining down reports and studies showing with harrowing detail and rigour how devastating our civilisation continued to be.

Decades of what I like to call 'sustainababble' had been unable to slow the onslaught of Empire. The face of Gaia was vanishing. Were efficient light bulbs ever going to be enough? Can technology really be expected to save us? What if consumer capitalism can't be fixed? What if capitalism is the crisis?

As we left the edge of the dam and sauntered aimlessly through the bush, we agreed that 'light green' environmentalism, despite the best of intentions, had more or less been co-opted by the market economy, entrenching business as usual at a time that was desperately in need of radical new ideas and an expanded ecological consciousness. What is needed, we said to each other, is action designed to unsettle or loosen the grip of the existing paradigm of 'sustainable development', and to show that a matrix of alternative worlds awaits those who are prepared to think otherwise and live alternatives into existence. Lived examples are the best antidote to despair, and that's an antidote always worth taking.

We concluded that experiments in sustainability shouldn't be about trying to do conventional development better; they should be about doing something other than conventional development. Similarly, the necessary revolution in the existing order of things should not be conceived of as some future event where a mobilised citizenry storms the Bastille – for Empire has no Bastille to storm anymore, its nodes of politico-financial power are so widely dispersed and decentralised that the system can evade a centralised confrontation of the old revolutionary kind.

No, the new revolution must be brought into the moment, into the present tense. We should not aim to destroy capitalism in the future but stop creating it, here and now, as best we can, knowing full well we are too often locked into reproducing it against our wishes. But we must try to break free and swim against the tide, no matter how futile it seems. Revolution should be conceived of as a way of life rather than a goal to be achieved.

For a time, Mortimer and I stood still in the midst of the bush, revelling in the unceasing eloquence of silence – a silence punctuated only with the diverse poetry of the wild. We had succeeded, if only for a few moments, in existing beyond capitalism. The thundering roar of a near-by freight train, however, soon broke our reverie, shaking the earth and reminding us how close we were to the coal-fired power stations that are the heart of industrial society. Ahh, the serenity!

For these reasons, we decided that creating a 'simpler way' demonstration site that was based upon a deeper green shade of environmental practice and a politics of grassroots activism was the most strategic use of our energies. We realised there wasn't much use campaigning for a progressive political party until there was a culture that was aware of the extent of the overlapping crises – a culture that was also able to imagine alternatives to the consumerist pattern of life and the growth economy, and to believe in those possibilities and desire them enough to make them a reality.

If we tried to act only at the household level, we'd surely become overwhelmed at the enormity of the task; if we waited for governments to act decisively, we'd be waiting forever. It followed that it was at the community and cultural levels where practical experiments in environmental living had most transformative potential. And if we failed to prefigure a sustainable way of life – a failure which we accepted as almost certain – then our efforts could at least be justified on the grounds of helping to increase local resilience in anticipation of forthcoming shocks and worsening crises.

But this raised the further question: was this project we were formulating just going to be another ecovillage? There would have been nothing wrong with that, of course. After all, few threads in the modern environmental movement have been more heroically active in building or trying to build new ways of living than the ecovillagers. In our discussions, however, Mortimer and I came to realise that there were two defining features of our envisioned project that would, if not distinguish it from the ecovillage movement, perhaps signal its evolution.

First of all, one of the main criticisms of ecovillages historically is that they have tended to be somewhat escapist or apolitical. We were not interested in merely creating a place where nice, disillusioned middle-class neo-hippies could come and have a lovely time growing their own organic veggies. We wanted the project to be explicitly political, engaged and inclusive, which is why we've tended to use the term 'demonstration project' rather than 'ecovillage' when describing what has emerged. Our aim was never to escape the system and live sustainably but to see if we could contribute to the positive transformation of the system. In this way, we hoped, the broader community could learn to live more sustainably and build resilience, not just a privileged few.

Secondly, we would seek to challenge the ecovillage movement in another sense too – by trying to radicalise it. One of the main concerns driving our project has been the uncomfortable realisation that even some of the world's most long-lasting and successful ecovillages have ecological footprints that are too high to be universalised. For example, in 2006 a study conducted of the Findhorn Ecovillage in Scotland, perhaps the most famous and inspiring ecovillage in the world, concluded that if everyone on the globe lived in ways similar to Findhorn, the planet would still be in ecological overshoot – we'd need one and a half planets. What this suggests is that even after many decades of the modern environmental movement, we still don't have many or any examples of what a flourishing 'one planet' existence might look like. Isn't that both interesting and disturbing?

How are we supposed to know in which direction we should be heading if we don't have a vision or example of where we'd like to end up? Before something can be brought deliberately into existence, first it must be envisioned.

This is the challenge humanity faces if we are to shape the future rather than merely be shaped by it. But once it has been envisioned, then the future must be built – even at the micro-scale, bit by bit – rather than merely dreamed of. By the time Mortimer and I returned to the edge of the dam, having circled the property, we had something of a meeting of minds about the contours of the project, even if we knew that the vision was vague and would inevitably evolve as it was put into practice. The first chapter of our new story was complete.

We had a project.

◆ ◆ ◆

The next chapter in this story was about actually getting started building this demonstration project. After our initial discussion on the edge of the dam in August 2013, and many more planning discussions with various people, our first project took place in December that year. We organised a natural building workshop, in which forty-two free-spirited people came to the property for a week to construct what is known as an 'earthship'.

The defining features of an earthship are, most famously, walls made from old car tyres that are rammed full of clay and then covered with render, and the whole structure is essentially dug into the side of a north-facing slope. Large north-facing glass doors, which we picked up from a tip shop, maximise the amount of winter sun the small earthship receives, and the thick earthen walls retain the heat in cooler temperatures. In the warmer months, the earthship stays cool from those very same thick earthen walls, assisted by a cooling pipe which runs twelve metres alongside the earthship under a couple of metres of clay. The cooling pipe works extremely well, like a non-electric air-conditioner.

By designing the building in this way, it needs neither heating in winter nor cooling in summer beyond what nature provides. As the permaculture philosophy implores, let's design our houses, our gardens, indeed, our communities, to work with nature, rather than against it. The lighting in the earthship is charged by a small solar panel, and is otherwise unconnected to further power sources.

It helps that the earthship also looks spectacular, with coloured bottle walls along the edges of its front face, successfully demonstrating that simplicity can be beautiful, like the stars in a night sky. What perfect economy! This isn't purely an aesthetic point; it is also pedagogical: by building 'out of this world' structures, it makes it easier to think 'beyond this world'. Sitting down for the first time in the peaceful sanctuary of the earthship, looking out over the property, I felt a heightened sense that other worlds were indeed possible. In February 2014, we organised another natural building workshop, this time to build a mud hut. Twenty-five people came to the property for a week, during which time we stomped on a lot of clay, sand, straw, and water to make the cob mixture, and had a deeply enriching time building a small but stunning cob cabin. Again, the thick earthen walls make the structure sufficiently cool in summer and warm in winter, without the need for external energy inputs. The windows again are orientated to the north according to passive solar design principles. All up, the build took a little over a week to finish and it cost just over $5,000.

It struck me at the time how pleasurable it was to be involved in building a small abode like this. I hold a doctorate in law, which arguably makes me one of the least practical people on earth – far too bookish for my own good – but there I was, with others similarly inexperienced in natural building, actually creating something real and amazing, in a community, using mainly the clay beneath our feet. There was a tangible vitality and energy to the project. I began to wonder whether the revolution might not be joyful.

Even more striking than the strange meaningfulness of the labour was how these workshops were showing themselves to be a way to escape the 'death grip' of a mortgage. If everyone in that workshop had stayed at the property for the year, we could have worked every other week and by December we could all have had such an abode. This should make us all think: if it is this easy, fulfilling and cheap to build with natural materials, why are we locked into such oppressively large mortgages? Something seems very wrong with today's social values and our property system if we are required to labour for forty years, in jobs we might not always find fulfilling, to pay for a high-impact conventional house when there are cheap and pleasurable alternatives that we, relatively unskilled laypeople, can build ourselves under the guidance of a couple of facilitators. It also highlights the importance of land access and affordability as an essential ingredient in any emancipatory project.

Later in 2014, we ran two more building workshops. First, in September, we built another small abode, this time using the 'earthbag' or 'superadobe' technique. This involves packing a long bag with clay and tamping it down firmly as a way to build the walls. On top of the layered earthbag walls we constructed a yurt-style octagon roof with reclaimed corrugated iron and wood. We insulated the roof with light earth (straw dipped into a clay slurry) and the interior ceiling was clad with wood from an old hardwood fence. The result was something that looked similar to a hobbit house straight out of Lord of the Rings. In December that year, we built a 'tiny house' out of salvaged timber and iron, taking twelve of us just over a week and costing under $2,500 in materials.

As well as these building projects, organic gardens on the property were expanding, a good-sized orchard was planted, water tanks and composting toilets had been installed, a yurt was erected, a large chicken and duck coop was built, a cob pizza oven was created, homemade beer was brewing, bees were buzzing, communities and networks were forming, and much, much more. Something very interesting was happening, even if we weren't exactly clear what it was.

In time we named the property Wurruk'an. Wurruk is the local Indigenous term meaning both 'Earth' and 'story'. K'an is the Mayan term for 'seed'. We invented the term Wurruk'an to signify our attempt to seed a new Earth story.

Around this time I got an email from a documentary maker, Jordan Osmond, who had come across our project on the internet and was interested in documenting the evolution of the property. By this stage we had developed some basic infrastructure on the property, so I had the idea that perhaps this was an opportunity to take the next step and see if there were more people who might be interested in coming out to live on the property on a permanent or semi-permanent basis, to explore practices of radical simplicity. The prospect of a documentary also meshed perfectly with our goal of reaching beyond our small node of resistance. We had created a crack in capitalism but now had to stick a crow bar into it and leverage our efforts. Here was an opportunity.

After speaking with Mortimer, who was sympathetic to the idea, I posted an invitation on a number of prominent permaculture and simple-living websites. We had decided to seek applications from people interested in forming a small community for the twelve months of 2015 in order to produce a 'simpler way' documentary that explored the living strategy of voluntary simplicity. We called it the Simpler Way Project. Our question: what might 'one planet' living look like?

Within a couple of weeks, we had received over fifty applications and began conducting interviews. The next chapter of our story was taking form. By early January 2015, there was a small community living on the property, having courageously thrown themselves into this evolving project, ready to pioneer and try to demonstrate a simpler way of life in the midst of industrial civilisation.

I write these words in December 2015, as the year's experiment draws to an end. It's been an incredibly educational and enriching journey, but by no means easy or without trial. We've achieved a huge amount and made lifelong friends, but we've also made our fair share of mistakes. I could say it's been like one of those rollercoaster rides that leaves you both thrilled and exhausted – proud that you were brave enough to go on the journey but unsure whether you'd journey quite the same way if you were to do it again. Here are a few reflections on the way of life that evolved and some of the challenges, delights, and lessons it produced.

When the community members arrived in January, they

either took up residence in one of the small abodes we had built, or built their own. One moved into a caravan and others, temporarily, into tents. There was a large, tin farm shed on the property, the back third of which got converted into a living and cooking space, with the front two thirds being a work shed. As the cooler months set in the shed arrangement was reversed, with the back third becoming the work shed and the front becoming the living space. It was insulated, beautifully clad with reclaimed wood and iron, and retrofitted with sinks and a wood burner oven and stove.

There was also a yurt that served as a secondary living space and, for a time, as an extra bedroom. As I noted earlier, there were basic composting toilets set up, gardens planted up with vegetables, and significant water tanks installed for drinking, cooking, and cleaning purposes. The property was also connected to the grid, so extra water was available when necessary.

The large and expanding gardens provided a good source of food, but by no means allowed for complete self-sufficiency. A significant amount of time was put into sourcing organic food as locally as possible, often purchasing in bulk, including a local, in-season veggie box. Dishes and clothes were washed by hand, and the community shared one fridge. None of the abodes were connected to the grid but small solar lights were available so that people had some light in the evenings.

Much of the furniture used was built by hand from wood that was lying around the property. One couple decided to build themselves a tiny house so they could move out of their tent, and did so successfully without expert guidance, using hand tools, for a grand expense of $420. Almost all the materials were salvaged from tip shops or skips on the side of the road, saving them from landfill. The final build for the year took place in October, when we ran a 'tiny house on wheels' workshop under the guidance of a wonderfully creative and generous carpenter. Like all the other workshops, it was a socially invigorating time during which we all developed our construction skills.

Even from this brief description, it's clear that the community was living in the tradition of the ecovillage movement, but seeking to push the boundaries of ecological practice a few steps further. Water and electricity consumption was minimal – a tiny fraction of the Australian average – due to simpler and communal ways of living. The small abodes (all around ten square metres) were built primarily with natural materials or with the waste streams of industrial society, and none had heating or cooling or even electricity beyond an off-grid solar light. Meals were cooked with local, fresh, organic food, and were almost always vegetarian. In the winter the community would often eat food that had been preserved in jars from the summer harvests. Some residents would dumpster dive, and when the conditions were right we could cook over a parabolic solar dish. Clothes were second-hand or hand-sewn, and we drank homemade beer, cider and mead – or water captured from the sky. Books and conversation replaced television, and superfluous consumer spending was more or less negligible.

The list of such practices could go on. The community authentically embraced the challenge of living a radically low-impact, low-energy way of life, and met with some real success. I'm not sure it achieved the ambitious target of 'one planet' living – it's a difficult thing to quantify – but I would be surprised if there are many ecovillages on the planet that have a smaller ecological footprint. In the material sense, life was simple but sufficient.

Accordingly, before reviewing some of the year's challenges and complexities, it is worth highlighting the achievements. Toward the end of the year, when visitors would come to Wurruk'an, I began to notice a mysterious sparkle in people's eyes as they would walk around the property for the first time. Perhaps those living at Wurruk'an had begun to take the spectacle of their existence for granted, but when visitors came to the property fresh from the hyper-consumerist, concrete jungle of Melbourne, their astonishment at what was going on could scarcely be disguised.

It seems that people are hungry for this type of project. People want to see the new world being built, new imaginaries realised in practice. It is a source of grounded hope. While I do not want to overstate the significance of Wurruk'an – it is but a drop in the ocean, and one still taking form – it nevertheless strikes me as embodying exactly the right strategy. In discussions about the woes of the world, I often find people quickly nodding in agreement, acknowledging the dire state of things. But all too often I then get the response, 'Yeah, but what's the alternative?' The value of demonstration projects like Wurruk'an is that they can broaden the horizons of what seems possible – and that is a gift not to be undervalued. To see that life can be otherwise is very energising and liberating.

When people come to Wurruk'an, I encourage them to imagine a world in which these types of projects enter the main-stream and are multiplied a million times over, not only in rural or semi-rural areas, but just as importantly within urban and suburban areas. This is the revolution of which I dream when I am awake. Wurruk'an by no means seeks to provide a blueprint that can be automatically applied independent of context. Not at all. Any such experiment with alternative ways of living can only take form in context-specific ways, meaning that we must all think creatively for ourselves. As the anti-capitalist slogan goes, there may be one 'no' but there are many 'yeses'. Radical simplicity in the city, therefore, will obviously look different to radical simplicity in the country, and will depend on innumerable other things, such as financial position, family size, weather patterns, and existing infrastructure. But Wurruk'an does debunk the Thatcherist dictum that 'there is no alternative'.

Most importantly, Wurruk'an provides a conception of sustainability beyond affluence, and that, I feel, is what the world needs more than anything else. Currently, the dominant strains in the environmental movement are aiming to universalise affluence in the hope of somehow making affluence sustainable through technological innovation and market mechanisms. But that's like trying to fit a square peg in a round hole – it can't be done. There is absolutely no way seven billion people can live in material affluence without collapsing ecosystems, to say nothing of the nine or ten billion people expected to inhabit Earth in coming decades. A 'fair share' ecological footprint is incompatible with material affluence, making affluence, I'm afraid to say, an illegitimate social goal.

This is, I acknowledge, a terribly unpopular thing to say. Nevertheless, the radical material simplicity of Wurruk'an is the currently unthinkable round peg we need in order to achieve what we all claim to want: a civilisation where the entire community of life can flourish within sustainable bounds. Wurruk'an is like a compass that can guide our efforts, a place where people can visit to reorientate themselves in a misguided world.

People will be quick, of course, to dismiss the endeavour as an escapist fantasy, just a bunch of Thoreauvian hippies who have retreated from the real world to live on the land in search of utopian isolation. It's an understandable critique, but ultimately one based on a superficial interpretation. If someone accepts that the changes necessary will never come from the 'top down', then the burden of resistance falls on individuals and communities, who must, as Gandhi implored, be the change they wish to see in the world. The fact that such action will typically seem small and insignificant does not for a moment mean that it implies a failure of strategy. (It's quite possible the best strategy will fail to achieve sustainability.)

In any case, the fact that prohibitively expensive land prices tend to push such oppositional experiments into rural areas does not mean that the spirit of opposition has no relevance to urban contexts. The message of Wurruk'an is not 'escape to the bush!' The message of Wurruk'an is far subtler: politics, as Aristotle argued, is always and necessarily founded upon a conception of the good life. Affluence is a flawed and inherently unsustainable conception; therefore, we need to found a politics upon a vision of material sufficiency for all. If people cannot see material sufficiency in action, this vision can't possibly be the foundation of a politics. Since a politics of sufficiency is necessary, Wurruk'an is justified. That, in short, is the logic of our project.

We also hope that our documentary will be used by activists to provoke a broader cultural conversation about these ideas, for not until there is a culture of sufficiency can we hold any hope for a politics of sufficiency.

Nevertheless, people shouldn't come to Wurruk'an looking

for all the answers – we might have some, but we certainly don't have them all. The real value of Wurruk'an and other such projects lie in their line of questioning: if globalising consumer affluence and maintaining limitless growth are recipes for ecological and thus humanitarian catastrophe, how can communities explore alternative, post-consumerist ways of living based on material sufficiency? How can we build highly localised, more self-sufficient economies, and thrive in doing so? Demonstration projects expand the imagination and allow these types of questions to breathe. Thus, when people come to Wurruk'an for a workshop or working bee, they inevitably develop themselves as they develop the property. Consequently, the person who comes is rarely the person who leaves. This is how cultures can change. This is how revolutions in consciousness are ignited – and how the fire spreads.

For all the many successes of the year, it would be disingenuous to deny or pass over the many challenges and compromises the community faced. Let me begin with the social dynamic. I've heard it said of ecovillages that anyone can build a mud house, grow organic food, and cook in a solar oven, but that the real challenge is the social one of living wisely in a community. After all, the history of intentional communities and ecovillages is, more or less, a history of social conflict, which has often led to breakdown and eventual dispersion. It seems our increasingly individualist culture has meant most of us have lost the skills of community living, which is hardly surprising. It is not a skill anyone is born with (despite what we might think); it is an art to be developed over a lifetime – rarely mastered, always demanding. These days, few people are trained in interpersonal skills.

This has never stopped people from trying to live well in communities. There seems to be something primordial about it, something human beings yearn for deeply, despite the challenges it inevitably brings. But it is worth acknowledging from the outset that community life is hard and participatory decision-making can be taxing, even if these things can also offer deep rewards.

It should come as no surprise, then, that the hardest part of the Simpler Way Project was the social aspect. Here was a community that formed for the purpose of the documentary, having never met each other before, linked only by the desire to explore a life of radical simplicity and to help raise awareness about the necessity of transcending consumer culture and its underlying growth fetishism. It has proven hard enough for the typical ecovillage or community to function socially, but this project had the added dimension of forming in such an unusual way, for such an unusual purpose, and for a limited timeframe. It was always going to be tough, we all knew that. And it was tough.

Nevertheless, there is a widespread sense that the social challenges have ultimately been enriching. Everyone is now a far wiser community member than when they arrived; everyone has developed as a social being. Throughout the year, the community explored the art of deep listening and learnt that that dialogue makes mutual demands on both listener and speaker. When a person expresses themselves bluntly or without due sensitivity, or feels strongly about an issue the group disagrees with, community members are being challenged to look beneath the tone of voice (perhaps the speaker is tired) and beneath the surface of the words (perhaps they're trying to say something else) to explore the potential for humane, enlightened compromise. Often, when we listen deeply, we see that conflict is not a result of unreasonable people being combative (although sometimes it is) but instead a result of reasonable people, with different concerns and priorities, not yet understanding each other. Community living calls on us to approach conflict in that spirit, with humility and open-mindedness, in the hope of muddling our way toward a workable compromise. The aim should not be to avoid conflict – that would be impossible. The aim is to deal with conflict wisely. In this respect, the year has been a year of progress.

From an ethical or philosophical perspective, one of the most interesting aspects of the year's living experiment was how the community struggled honourably with the question of balancing principle and pragmatism. In one of the big-picture discussions held early in the year, one of the community members made the striking comment that 'if I were to live and consume strictly in accordance with my ethics of sustainability and justice, I'd die'. It's a disconcerting realisation. We live in a world that so often locks us into ways of living that we know are unjust or unsustainable. One might know that driving is a leading cause of climate change, yet in the absence of good bike lanes or public transport, getting to work is more or less impossible. One might despise the unethical business strategies of the big supermarkets, yet often find their convenience just too seductive. One might be perfectly aware that billions around the world are desperately hungry, yet find oneself casually throwing out food. No doubt, everyone has their own contradictions they try to live with. I certainly have my own.

Out at Wurruk'an, these contradictions were often brought to the surface and critically analysed. One of the things that inspired me most about the community was that the conversations were always real. Owing to that honesty, however, the community soon discovered how muddy the waters of ethical living actually are.

This is not to say that since ethics are ambiguous, we can keep on consuming mindlessly. It is just to acknowledge that no one is innocent in a world that makes truly ethical consumption all but impossible. At every turn, our consumption practices are tainted with fossil fuels, exploitative labour, and the blood of others. But we must try to escape those contaminations, and do everything we can to avoid supporting them with our actions and spending habits. Most importantly, we need to begin building a new economy that is not grounded upon such things. But to some extent it seems we are all implicated in a globalised economy that tragically prohibits ethical living. We are all different shades of injustice, a point designed not to induce guilt but to engender increased humility, care, and kindness.

Put otherwise, my point is that the community at Wurruk'an has not been comprised of eco-saints but human beings. Some pushed the boundaries of ecological practice more than others – and they are to be admired for challenging us to challenge ourselves. But at various stages, for various reasons, everyone found themselves making certain ethical compromises. This is life in industrial civilisation. Exploring simplicity in an overly complex society is riddled with contradictions and challenges. So much for voluntary simplicity. Sustainable consumption rather implies involuntary complexity. This is one of the many paradoxes of the simple life.

As this chapter of the Simpler Way Project comes to close, it is clear that the book of Wurruk'an is not yet complete – perhaps, by its very nature, it can never be completed. No doubt there will be more twists in the tale as our uncertain and ever-changing future bears down upon us. For now, let me take this opportunity to thank the brave pioneers who threw themselves into this mad but noble experiment. Their integrity and authenticity have been beyond question, even if it has become increasingly clear that sustainability is a process not a destination.

As artist-activist John Jordan says: 'When we are asked how we are going to build a new world, our answer is: "We don't know, but let's build it together".' If we start in that spirit, we are off on the right foot.

◆ ◆ ◆

The creative task of managing our civilisational descent – daunting though it is – promises to be both meaningful and fulfilling, provided we are prepared to let go of dominant conceptions of the good life and begin telling ourselves new stories of prosperity. Consumerism was an experiment that failed. It led us down a dead end. Only by letting go – or, rather, only by ripping ourselves free – can we transcend it.

Mercifully, there is a door hidden in the wall, providing us with an escape route if only we are prepared to embrace the unfashionable values of sufficiency, frugality, mindfulness, appropriate technology, self-governance, and local economy. Needless to say, personal action alone is not enough. We must also build structures that support a more localised, simpler way to live, and this can only be achieved through the collective genius and power of community action. Together we must write a new future, an undertaking that has already begun as individuals and communities begin to build the new world within the shell of the old.

We should explore alternatives not because we are ecologically compelled to live differently – although we are – but because we are human and deserve the opportunity to flourish with dignity, within sustainable bounds. This does not mean regressing to something prior to consumerism; rather, it means drawing on the wisdom of ages to advance beyond consumerism, in order to produce something better, freer, and more humane – even if it will also be more humble. This revolution, no doubt, will require all the wisdom, creativity, and compassion we can muster. But impossible things have happened before. And if we fail, may we fail with dignity.

As John Holloway writes: 'We need no promise of a happy ending to justify our rejection of a world we feel to be wrong.'

Let us declare, in chorus, that providing 'enough, for everyone, forever' is the defining objective of a just and sustainable world, a world that we should try to build by working together in free association. And let us show that material sufficiency in a free society provides the conditions for an infinite variety of meaningful, happy, and fulfilling lives. For embracing a 'simpler' way of life does not mean hardship or going back to the Stone Age. It means focusing on what is sufficient to live well, and discovering that the good life does not consist in the accumulation of 'nice things'. Just enough is plenty.

Thus our defining challenge is to seek out and embody the 'middle way' between over-consumption and under-consumption, where basic material needs are sufficiently met but where attention is then redirected away from superfluous material pursuits, in search of non-materialistic sources of satisfaction and meaning. Those sources are abundant – inexhaustible – if only we knew it. It is time to abandon affluence and turn to the realm of the spirit to satisfy our hunger for infinity.

It is painfully clear, of course, that governments around the world are not interested in moving 'beyond growth' or questioning consumer culture, and there are few signs of things changing at the top. Empire, we can be sure, will not contemplate its own self-annihilation; nor will it lie down like a lamb at the mere request of the environmental movement. Empire will struggle for existence all the way down.

It follows that the transformation that is needed must emerge 'from below', driven into existence by diverse, inspired and imaginative social movements that seek to produce a post-capitalist society. What role will you play? It is a question with no generalisable answer. However we answer it, we must endeavour to live our alternative worlds into existence, here and now, and show them to be good, while at the same time recognising that the great transition that is needed will likely come only at the end of a rough road – after or during a series of crises. Can we turn the crises of our times into opportunities for civilisational renewal? That is the question, the challenge, posed by our turbulent moment in history.

In the words of Theodore Roszak, author of *Where the Wasteland Ends*:

> There is one way forward: the creation of flesh and blood examples of low-consumption, high quality alternatives to the mainstream pattern of life. This we can see happening already on the counter-cultural fringes. And nothing – no amount of argument or research – will take the place of such living proof. What people must see is that ecologically sane, socially responsible living is good living; that simplicity, thrift and reciprocity make for an existence that is free.

Our task, therefore, is to expose and better understand the myths that dominate our destructive and self-transforming present, and to envision what life would be like, or could be like, if we were to liberate ourselves from today's myths and step into new ones. We search for grounded hope between naive optimism and despair. Without vision and defiant positivity, we will perish.

Unfortunately, our myths today have become so entrenched that they have assumed a false necessity, which is to say, they no longer seem to be myths at all. Rather, the myths of industrial civilisation – which are the myths of limitless growth, techno-logical redemption, and fulfilment through affluence – seem to be a reflection of some 'grand narrative' from which we cannot escape.

But there is a collective rumbling in the world today. Do you hear it? It is spreading in all directions, which means it is both coming your way and emanating from you. Currently dormant, our repressed hopes are all embers ready to ignite, awaiting a rush of oxygen that will flare our utopian ambitions. Breathe deeply, they say, and demand the impossible. Let us stoke the fire of ecological democracy that is burning in our eyes, not because we think we will succeed in producing a just and sustainable world, but because if we do not try, something noble in our hearts and spirits will be lost. So open your mind, gentle reader, for the future is but clay in the hands of our imaginations.

We are being called to make things new.

OTHER BOOKS FROM
THE SIMPLICITY INSTITUTE

Just Enough is Plenty: Thoreau's Alternative Economics (2016)
Samuel Alexander

Deface the Currency: The Lost Dialogues of Diogenes (2016)
Samuel Alexander

Sufficiency Economy: Enough, for Everyone, Forever (2015)
Samuel Alexander

Prosperous Descent: Crisis as Opportunity in an Age of Limits (2015)
Samuel Alexander

Simple Living in History: Pioneers of the Deep Future (2014)
edited by Samuel Alexander and Amanda McLeod

The Hidden Door: Mindful Sufficiency as an Alternative to Extinction
(2013) Mark A. Burch

Entropia: Life beyond Industrial Civilisation (2013)
Samuel Alexander

FOR MORE INFORMATION, SEE THE SIMPLICITY INSTITUTE

www.simplicityinstitute.org